WASTE AS RESOURCE, BY DESIGN

WASTE AS RESOURCE, BY DESIGN

3rd International Conference on Design

February 16th, 2018

Editors

PROF. SASI GOPAL MENON

MS. KOSHALPREET KAUR

DR. ANJALI AGRAWAL

BLOOMSBURY

NEW DELHI • LONDON • OXFORD • NEW YORK • SYDNEY

BLOOMSBURY INDIA
Bloomsbury Publishing India Pvt. Ltd
Second Floor, LSC Building No. 4, DDA Complex, Pocket C – 6 & 7,
Vasant Kunj, New Delhi 110070

First published in 2018

ISBN: 978-93-87471-79-5

2 4 6 8 10 9 7 5 3 1

Typeset by Fortune Graphics, New Delhi

Printed and bound in India by Replika Press Pvt Ltd

Contents

Preface

In a short span of time, GD Goenka University has established itself as one of the leading private universities in North India. With a student base that is drawn from across the country and faculty with experience in both academics and industry, the university provides an excellent platform to nurture skills and attitudes that can propel the new generation to take on future challenges. The School of Fashion & Design has been at the forefront of this movement and through it's various initiatives, has been successfully impacting the creation of a body of professional designers who are increasingly being sought after by the creative industries. The conference on design, CODE, is an annual platform through which the school demonstrates it's commitment to addressing issues of relevance and bringing together likeminded people and participating in dialogue that has strategic importance and impactful result. This year, CODE 2018 attempts to address the very important and highly critical issue of waste that is increasingly impacting our day-to-day life, our environment as well as our sustainability cycle. Waste is being produced by industry, discarded by consumers and left to kill our fragile planet. This linear cycle is wreaking havoc with our ecology, weather, and natural systems and is now at a tipping point. The anthropocene era has raised more questions about the planet than it has produced answers. It is therefore high time that we work constructively towards addressing the issue from a holistic perspective. While many efforts are being done across the world, there is an urgent need to create the right kind of networks and synergize these efforts for larger impact. CODE 2018 attempts to start a long-term dialogue with various stakeholders at the local and national levels and pave the way for a future plan that can be translated into action. The School of Fashion & Design aims to play a pivotal role as a think tank and experimentation ground for endeavors in this arena. The papers presented in this book contain various viewpoints regarding the subject and I hope this will bring the dialogue to a larger audience of academics and professionals and encourage them to work with us towards arriving at sustainable solutions that can have long term impact.

Sasi Gopal Menon
Dean, School of Fashion & Design
GD Goenka University

Acknowledgements

Organizing an International Conference and compiling the proceedings is a challenging task accomplished by the continuous support, hard work and dedication of team of G D Goenka University. I would like this opportunity to express my gratitude to everyone who made this possible.

We are grateful to Mr. Nipun Goenka, Managing Director, G D Goenka Group for his encouragement and support in organizing an event of this scale. We would like to extend our heartfelt gratitude to Prof. (Dr.) Shri Hari, Vice Chancellor G D Goenka University (GDGU) for his valuable guidance, support and advice in making the conference a great success. We are appreciative to our distinguished speakers who accepted our invitation to share their knowledge, experience and expertise with the delegates and students contributing immensely to the success of the event. We are also extremely grateful to our authors and researchers, who chose to share their research at this conference. We, however, regret and extend our sincere apologies to researchers whose papers could not be included in this compilation.

We would like to express our gratitude to our reputed publisher, Bloomsbury and their team, for their patience and support to the timely publication of this book.

We are greatly indebted to our sponsors for their encouragement and support to the success of this conference.

Finally, we would like to thank the faculty, officers and staff members at G D Goenka University and all the professors and team members from our academic partners Politecnico Di Milano in extending their support for CODE. We owe a special thanks to the organizing committee, conference coordinators, faculty, staff and students of the School of Fashion and Design (SOFD) for making the conference a huge success.

Energy Grid Transport System
Breathe in Breathe Out Cities

AJAY SINGH BISHT
School of Fashion and Design, G D Goenka University, Gurgaon, India

ABSTRACT

While seeking micro level solution, one should not ignore its place in the larger scheme of things. If we consider the macro concept properly before seeking micro solutions, then the chances of shortsightedness and negative spillovers of the solution are reduced.

Similarly, although this paper is a future car design concept idea, understanding the background and macro environment within which our solution is embedded is essential.

Each time we try to replace an old model by a better one, more often than not, we seem to hurt the planet even more. To ensure that we find lasting solutions with minimal side effects, we will have to concentrate more on parameters, considerations and process of finding solutions, rather than the solution itself. If we manage to ensure minimum unintended disruptions in the short and the long run, our solutions will have a definite positive impact.

IDEA – The entire city roads will be covered by electric grid channels, and through these channels, the energy generated by the interaction of the vehicles with its environment, will either be used to power the vehicle or will be sent back to central city grid in case of excess capacity. The energy generation process will integrate all the possible technologies with the aim of balancing the energy output and input as much as possible.

Keywords: *Energy grid, Transport system, Unifying the goals, Perennial supply.*

INTRODUCTION

With Global warming, climate change and pollution threatening the planet like never before, it is race against time for us to get our act together. But as history tells us, each time we have tried to replace an old model by a better one, more often than not, we seem to hurt the planet even more.

It is quite possible that the human population size combined with its high consuming, energy guzzling lifestyle, is not sustainable at all, and a global catastrophe is inevitable, creating a better people to resource ratio. But neither can we cut down human population size drastically, nor can we alter the way billions of people live, think and behave suddenly. We have come this far evolving over millenniums, and we can't change in a few decades. But we can certainly ask ourselves a few reasonable questions. Are we doing the best we can? How can we avoid mistakes of the past so that our approach is not piecemeal in nature? Holistic approach is the only way forward to provide lasting solutions.

There is no doubt that the problem begins with overpopulation creating immense pressure on the finite resources of the planet and is further accentuated by our short term solutions to various desires, needs and requirements. The irony is that, individual solutions are often contradictory to needs of the society, solutions for one society often cause suffering for another and short term solutions are often disasters in the long run. That is why none of the solutions created by us seem to achieve the desired potential over a significant area and time. We tend to solve one problem while creating numerous side effects – some visible, mostly invisible.

At one time with limited population, the Earth had the capacity to absorb the human impact and replenish the resources efficiently. But today, Earth can't replenish our footprints easily and instead, alters itself in terms of temperature patterns, weather patterns, ocean levels and currents, water level and quality, patterns of natural phenomena leading to catastrophic disasters, and composition of land, air and water- all of which create new threats to human life every day.

No matter where we start from, primary cause of the real major global crisis created by man is the need for energy. Although, the problem of rapid population growth began as soon as we settled down and developed agriculture, but the Earth still had the capacity to fulfill our basic needs without too much strain. But recent history of rapid technological advancements and fast changing lifestyle, created need for immense energy-fulfillment of which is really devastating the planet.

Today, while on one hand, we are at one of the worst times in the history of mankind in terms of threat to the planet, on the other hand, our lifestyle choices have destroyed most of the safeguards that our ancient cultures created to protect the nature. But surprisingly, our best hope lies in the very factor that played a major role, many times indirectly, in bringing us to this dismal state- technology. Today, any hope of significant and feasible solution, will undoubtedly, has to come through technology.

THE PARAMETERS AND CONSIDERATIONS FOR A SUSTAINABLE FUTURE SOLUTION

To ensure that we find lasting solutions with minimal side effects, we will have to concentrate more on parameters, considerations and process of finding solutions, rather than the solution itself. If we manage to ensure minimum unintended disruptions in the short and the long run, our solutions will have a definite positive impact, no matter how small. To make sustainability solutions work over long period, we must keep a few things in mind:

Transcending Time and Place

The solutions we create need to have an organic life of their own. They should be able to start small, to test the waters and then be expandable into further avatars over different cultures, locations, walks of life, technological advancements and economic models. Solutions should dig deep into the future – they should be relevant from today to another few centuries. If we don't have the foresight and are unable to look beyond a particular area, time and culture, the solutions will be a short term thought process and will ignore deeper complications. Furthermore, once they run out of gas, we will be again running around trying to rectify their residual complications and finding new solutions.

Uniting the Goals

Each time we alter a way of life for betterment, certain amount of friction is developed by the society, reducing its effectiveness. It is important that our solutions should help individual, community, country and the planet simultaneously. Only by minimizing conflict of interest, we will be able to ensure minimum side effects to the solutions. Only by minimizing side effects will we be able to achieve full potential of our solutions.

Integration with Other Solutions

Most of the time, the initial work done and foreseen by the solutions, is well overshadowed by the infinite ripples it causes deep into future, over long distances and towards totally unconnected walks of life.

So the flexibility becomes the key, as they should be able to blend with different models of economic and social structures, creating a positive ripple effect in multiple directions. Easy blending ability with different infrastructures, partially or fully, makes the solution much more effective and acceptable.

Non-perishable Resource

If we want to make our energy solutions last really long, we should only tap into resources which are nonperishable. Solar energy, wind energy, geo thermal energy, tidal and wave energy are some of the resources that are truly abundant in nature and we are already tapping into them. But all of them have an extraction limit.

So a better idea for endless supply is, 'breathe in and out' system of tapping energy. Since energy is never destroyed and only converted into other forms, theoretically, it can always be reused. If the energy release from one process is used by the other, it can create a perennial loop of unending and clean energy supply- as long as the energy is being used, it will be created at the same time.

With advance technologies of future and minimal conversion loss, we should be able to make this idea a reality one day. In such a scenario, the current renewable sources like solar, wind, geothermal, and ocean energies will only be used to fulfill the conversion loses.

Conventional Wisdom

Even when we look for new guidelines on how to frame our solutions, we cannot ignore the basic criteria on which all energy solutions are based. We will have to consider resulting air, water, thermal, chemical and radioactive pollution, the cost in terms of health and mortality, the energy footprint, the space utilization, the water consumption, the reliability, the safety and continuity of the technology, and finally the impact on land and wildlife.

THE CORE IDEA

The entire city is covered by a system of electric grid channels, embedded into the roads, which power all vehicles and the energy generated by internal and external interactions of the vehicle is tapped into, and the excess power is sent back to the center city grid. Each vehicle has two flexible and stretchable extensions which are magnetically attached to the electric channels whenever they come near them, and are detached as soon as they move away. One extension charges the battery to keep it full, while the other sends the power back to the grid in case of excess. The technologies involved in on board energy creation, cover every possible option of energy generation-wind, heat, motion, solar and friction.

The ultimate aim is to create a system which takes care of the ultimate waste generated by a highly dense, rapidly growing and consumerist populace- energy. Another way to look at it is that, no waste is generated by energy creation and application. If this idea can be extended to other walks of life, the ultimate goal will be to develop breath in breath out city systems, where energy consumption will directly feed into energy waste.

THE CONCEPT CAR DESIGN AND TECHNOLOGIES

Accommodating all the ideas and the parameters, the resulting car design will have the following features:

The Energy Exchange

The car will have two flexible and stretchable extensions on the bottom of the car- one to send energy and one to receive energy from the electric channels on the roads. These extensions will attach themselves to the channels loosely as soon they detect a channel and will start forming an equilibrium state for energy optimization. As soon as the car drifts away from the channel, the extensions will detach. Energy will be exchanged from car to the channels as per requirement. Depleted battery will receive energy from the central city grid. In case of stationary car or excess energy generation by various on board mechanisms, the car will send extra energy back to the city grid.

The Integration of Technologies

The idea is to integrate all technologies of saving and generating power in each and every vehicle.

Solar Power Generation

The entire car will be painted with "Solar Paint", which will harness the solar power as per availability. While the solar power will charge battery, it will be used to provide and sell excess power back to the city grid. Since cars are parked in the sun most of the times during the daytime, unused solar energy will be harnessed in abundance.

Researchers from the Royal Melbourne Institute of Technology have developed a paint that can generate hydrogen fuel from moist air and sunlight. The team expects the technology to be ready in five years. According to a report on RMIT's website, the

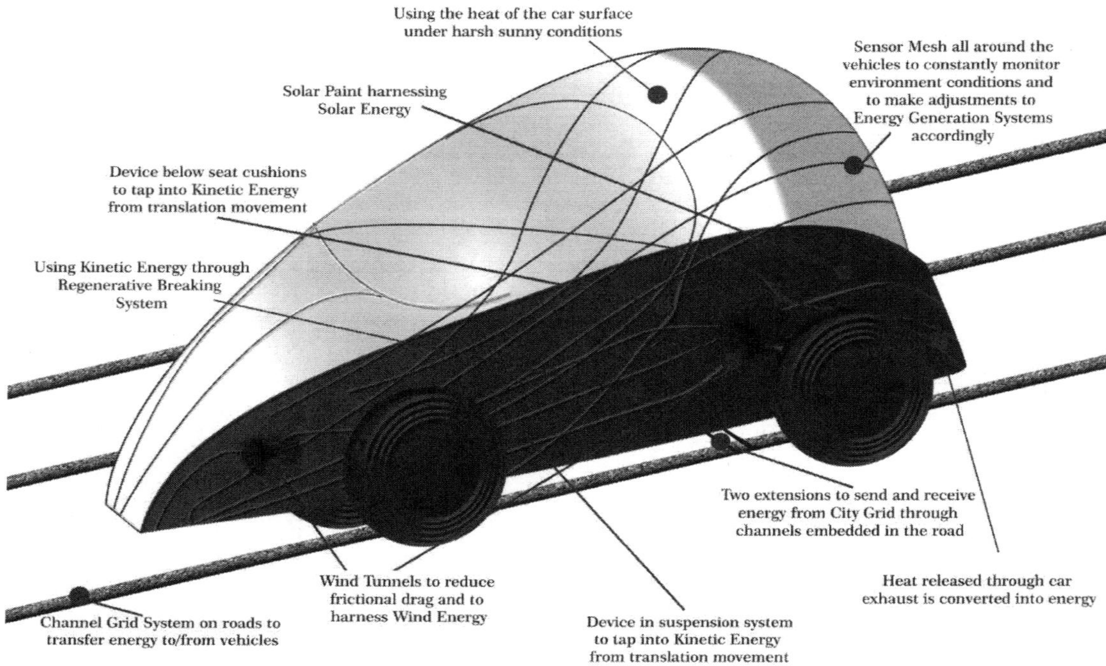

material absorbs solar energy as well as moisture from the surrounding air. It can then split the water into hydrogen and oxygen, collecting the hydrogen for use in fuel cells or to power a vehicle. "*The simple addition of the new material can convert a brick wall into energy harvesting and fuel production real estate*," explained lead researcher Dr. Torben Daeneke.

The technology for use of Solar Paint in vehicles is still a few years away, but it is being developed and will be ready for practical application in near future. Once we reach that stage, we can further develop ways to use 'Concentrated Solar Power' at small scale, which is highly unfeasible right now due to the cost involved.

Wind Energy Generation and Reducing Wind Drag

Harnessing the wind energy in vehicles is a huge subject of debate. How can we use wind energy without increases the frictional drag on the car?

According to paper titled, "*Electric Vehicles with Charging Facility using Wind Energy*", presented in World Renewable Energy Congress 2011, Sweden, "*if wind energy is used to extract some power in such a way that it does not create any component of force or thrust opposite to the direction of the propulsion of the vehicle, then this gained energy can be used to produce electricity to charge up the battery of the electric vehicle itself. At the same time drag can be expected to be reduced by passing this air to the rear side (Low pressure side) of the vehicle. Air stream sliding over the body of the vehicle cannot enter into the rear side due to vortex shedding. If air streams are allowed to flow in this region by any means then the form drag will be reduced by some amount and at the same time it may be possible to generate electricity using the kinetic energy of wind.*"

Another idea they proposed was, "*As the vehicle moves forward, it lefts the air stream behind. A turbulence or disturbance is created on the wind when a vehicle moves through it. If stationary wind turbines are placed near the road then energy can be extracted from the wind stream generated due to the movement of the vehicle. Such a study had been carried out in University of Arizona by a group of students.*"

When we are creating an inter dependent energy biosphere, then it becomes essential that we try to harness the energy which vehicles create all around them, either through wind, motion, friction or heat. There have been various attempts at using the wind energy to power vehicles without any significant outcome. A wind powered Formula AE sport car by RORMaxx was one such attempt.

We don't know how long it will take to develop a feasible technology to use wind energy, but we can definitely create wind tunnels, passing through the car, to reduce the frictional drag, reducing need for energy. These channels will not reduce the strength of the car below safety standards. Ultimately, all energy saved can be looked upon as additional energy generated.

Use of Motion/Kinetic Energy

Kinetic energy is one of the energies which is already being used successfully in Electric Vehicles. When the vehicles break to stop or slow down, the inertia of the vehicles creates energy which is stored in batteries using regenerative breaking system. In fact, heavier the vehicle, more the inertia and thus more is the energy generated. That is why, heavy duty trucks have 25 times more kinetic energy than a typical car travelling at the same speed.

Another idea is to utilize the contact between ground and wheel, which induces translation movement. This dynamics can be converted into energy by putting a device in the suspension system of the car. In fact, bumpier the road more energy will be generated through gravity, motion and inertia interaction.

Theoretically, same translation movement energy can be captured by putting devices in the seat cushions of the car or on the base plate of the car which support the whole body or the tires of the car – wherever there is a constant translational motion.

Use of Heat

Only about one third of the potential energy in the fuel for propulsion is used and the remaining is lost as waste heat. If we are able to tap into this wasted energy, we will have far more fuel efficient vehicles.

But at present thermoelectric materials which convert heat into electricity are highly inefficient. Since a lot of work is going in this field, we are sure to make a better use of heat in near future.

ADVANTAGES OF THE SYSTEM

Weight and Charging Solution

There is no doubt that in terms of sustainability, Battery Electric Vehicles are way ahead then any of the solutions we have come up with. But the extra weight of the battery, which limits the mileage upon a single charge, is a huge drawback. Constant charging will definitely reduce the need to carry extra weight as battery. Since this will also make stationary charging totally redundant, it will solve another problem of long time that it takes to charge a battery.

Balancing Supply and Boosting Renewables

One of the major drawbacks of most of the renewable sources like solar, wind and waves is that their supply is not constant and it is not easy to match demand and supply of energy during variable production. But, if all the vehicles are connected to the central grid, they can provide a great buffer supplying energy to the city – they almost become a giant collective storage device. This will give a great boost to other renewable energy resources also. A lot of environmental benefits of Battery Electric Vehicles depend upon the source of energy. By helping the renewable resources, will make it most sustainable.

Self Regulating Mechanism

By creating a buffer storage capacity, we will reduce the need for smart charging and constant monitoring of the city energy supply. It will become a self-sustaining entity to a great extent.

Cleaner Battery Use

By reducing the need for increased battery capacity, we will have longer lasting batteries. To a certain extent, this will address the problem of recyclability of the battery and the harm caused to the environment during mining for battery metal.

Lower Transportation Cost

Eliminating the need for transportation for energy such as fossil fuel or hydrogen will hugely reduce the cost of energy, and also reducing the transportation vehicles will lead to lesser vehicle density and cleaner environment.

Minimizing Energy Production Need

This concept will use and make energy at the same time and will almost eliminate the need to deplete nature and pollute air.

Healthier, Happier, Safer and Harmonious Society

We can't overemphasize the effect of this system on the mental and physical health of the people. Grid system will discourage lane changing, rash driving, and traffic violations while improving safety, traffic monitoring and research and policing, thereby calming the traffic chaos. Better safety, smoother traffic, lesser noise and air pollution will create healthier, happier and thriving societies.

Furthermore, by encouraging people to use common grid instead of individual batteries/fuel, they will feel more stake in the community. It will be beneficial for people to keep community harmonious and they will always feel connected as they are always receiving and giving back at the same time. We will create the same belonging to community which we once went felt through the Nature.

Better Driverless Cars

Improved lane driving and connection of all vehicles to the central grid most of the time, will make driverless cars an easier possibility.

Minimizing Transmission and Distribution Losses

This grid system will reduce the need for large power plants and long distance power transmissions need. Small areas will be self-sustainable in terms of energy needs and will need only small power generation capacity to cover conversion loses. It will cut down transmission and distribution loses drastically.

Safety against Blackouts and Catastrophic Accidents

Micro self-sustainable grids will make large scale area power blackouts a history. It will also drastically reduce the possibility of a large scale disaster such as nuclear reactor explosion, bursting of a hydro power dam or a deep water oil spill.

MAJOR HURDLES IN DEVELOPING THE SYSTEM

Integration of Technologies

The biggest problem we will face in the vehicle grid system idea is the integration of various technologies. Apart from solar and kinetic energy used to generate power in vehicles, where we have achieved some degree of success, we are still struggling to harness the energy efficiently in other areas such as motion, wind and heat. Once we develop these advance technologies in future, it will be a very tough task to bring them together. Since their development is not taking place keeping their future integration in mind, we will need to rework on all the technologies to bring them together.

The Energy Exchange in Flexible Motion

Until now we have two ways of powering a vehicle- either we fuel up a stationary vehicle (in almost all the cases), or provide power to a vehicle running on particular track (trains and trams). Exploring the possibility of give and take of energy in a fast and flexible motion is a totally new field of study. The feasibility of this technology or alternate solution will form the basis of the practicality of this idea.

Complete Overhaul Of Infrastructure

Another major hurdle is that, almost all our infrastructure will become outdated. Altering each and every road will be a logistical nightmare and an extremely expensive proposition.

Storage

The efficiency of the system will require an adequate storage capacity of energy to minimize wastage. Today we have various technologies to store energy such a Solid state batteries, Flow batteries, Flywheels, Compressed air energy storage, Thermal storage, Pumped Hydro Power, Chemical energy storage, Capacitors and Super Conducting Magnetic Energy Storage. We have the technology, but its capacity is really small at present.

IHS, the respected energy consultancy, projects that energy storage will grow from a one-third of a GW in 2013 to 6 GW by 2017 and more than 40 GW by 2022. In 2013, McKinsey estimated that the economic impact of energy storage would be at least $90 billion a year by 2025, and possibly much more (up to $635 billion) depending on how fast it is applied to cars. This is a drop in the bucket that is the $6 trillion global energy market.

Efficiency

When we are dealing with two way flow of energy and multiple energy generation process integration, efficiency decides the value of the process. Energy is lost each time we transmit or convert energy.

For example, only about 20% of the energy is used for propulsion of cars in comparison to the input energy. And according to The World Bank, the electric power transmission and distribution loss average of the world was 8.2% in 2014.

We will have to achieve new levels of energy technology efficiency to ensure that so many layers of transfer and conversion of energy make any sense at all.

CONCLUSION

It is important to understand that the idea of the concept vehicle is so farfetched in terms of current and foreseeable technological developments, that it doesn't seem feasible at all. It might take another few decades for us, to even start thinking about working on it. It might take more decades to come up with a decent prototype. But, though it might take a lot of time to make it work, it will be worth it, as the solutions it will create, will really have a huge implications running deep into our future goals.

Furthermore, it will be just the beginning of the idea. It will be expanded into all facets of life – from houses to offices to public spaces to recreational zones. Entire cities will breathe in and out together. All manmade creation will achieve the same balance as the nature in terms of energy interdependence. Imagine whole cities surface becoming a giant solar and wind energy generator, or every nook and corner of the city is generating power each time something moves or heats up. Ultimately there won't be any need for power plants at all.

REFERENCES

[1] Caughill, P. (2017). 'A New "Solar Paint" Lets You Transform Your Entire House into a Source of Clean Energy'.

[2] Ferdous, S.M., Khaled, W.B., Benozir, A., Salehin, S., Ovy, E.G. (2011). 'Electric Vehicles with Charging Facility using Wind Energy', by World Renewable Energy Congress, Sweden.

[3] Blanco, S. (2009). 'More Details on RORMaxx Formula AE Wind Assisted Car'.

[4] Nasser, H. (2013). 'Vehicle Dynamics Conversion into Power (Dynapower)', published in Science Direct.

[5] (2009). 'New Energy's Technology for Generating Electricity from Motion of Heavy Vehicles Doubles Energy Capture', published in Solar Window.

[6] Blanco, S. (2017). 'Electric Cars Win on Energy Efficiency vs Hydrogen, Gasoline, Diesel: Analysis', published in Green Car Reports.

[7] Rodrigo, P. (2017). 'Research Seeks to Turn Waste Engine Heat into Power'.

[8] Nyquist, S. (2015). 'How Energy Storage could Change Everything about Renewables'.

Utilization of Waste Teak Leaves (*Tectona grandis*) for Sustainable Dyeing of Selected Natural and Synthetic Fabrics

AKSHITA AGRAWAL[1] AND SHEETAL CHOPRA[2]

[1] *Research Scholar, Department of Fabric and Apparel Science, Lady Irwin College, University of Delhi, Delhi, India*

[2] *Assistant Professor, Department of Fabric and Apparel Science, Lady Irwin College, University of Delhi, Delhi, India*

E-mail: akshita2512ag@gmail.com; sheetal_chopra@hotmail.com

ABSTRACT

*It is a common practice to prune the tree branches to improve wood quality thus leaves are easily available as by product from pruning and also from wood harvesting. In the present study, waste Teak leaves (Tectona grandis) were utilized for the extraction of dye. The conditions of application of extracted dye have been optimized on wool, silk and nylon fabrics. In the present study, the characterization of the inorganic component of teak leave was done in terms of moisture and ash content. Extraction of dye was carried out in aqueous medium at acidic, neutral and alkaline pH. The extracted dye was also characterized in terms of yield%. Dyeing was carried out using pre-mordanting method followed by post-mordanting with 10% (owf) of eleven selected mordants. The dyed samples were analysed for their colour values in terms of K/S and L*c*h*/L*a*b* values and were assessed for their fastness properties such as wash, rub, light and perspiration fastness as per the ISO and ASTM standards.*

Various combinations of the mordants result in obtaining pleasing and harmonious colours which were used to create designs using mordanting and printing with extracted dye.

A design catalogue of combinations of dyed and printed stoles and dupattas of silk were prepared and from this catalogue some designs were developed for final product.

Keywords: *Teak leaves, Antimicrobial properties, Waste utilization, Sustainable dyeing.*

INTRODUCTION

Growing consciousness about organic value of sustainable products has generated renewed interest of consumers towards using textiles dyed with eco-friendly dyes.

Waste utilization has become an effective way for the promotion of sustainable technologies and processing methods. Approximately 70% of all the dyes being used by the Indian Textile Industry are azo dyes [1]. The use of natural products for imparting antimicrobial properties on textile materials has also been widely researched [2].

Teak is a valuable tropical timber species produced in industrial plantation in more than 43 countries. National and international demand for teak timber exceeds the sustainable yield from plantations. In India about 2,76,000 hectare area is involved in the cultivation of Teak trees and every year around 400 million of trees are being cut for the wood to be used for furniture and the leaves get wasted. These waste leaves can be used in various ways and we can get wealth from waste material [3]. Flavonoids in teak leaves are responsible for its medicinal properties such as antibacterial, antioxidant, cytotoxic, antifungal, hypoglycemic, anti-inflammatory, diuretic, anti-asthmatic, anti-bronchitis, analgesic, anti-pyretic, anti-diabetic, anthelmintic and many more [4].

Dye can be extracted from waste teak leaves and the residual portion can be used as bio-fertilizers. These dyes are eco-friendly and have no allergic action on skin like synthetic dyes. More over the procedure is very cost effective and can be a good idea for a small scale industry or a medium scale industry.

Natural dyes are similar to disperse dye in terms of relatively low molecular mass, low solubility and no strong solubilizing groups [5]. The literature review showed a similar structure of teak leaves and that there is a possibility of extraction of colour from teak leaves but not much work has been done on its application on synthetic textile material [6], [7], [8], [9], and 10]. The antimicrobial properties of the dyed fabrics have also not been assessed so far. The focus of recent researches is also on finding ways of making the processing as sustainable as possible.

The present study is an attempt to optimize the procedure of extraction of dye and apply it on selected natural and synthetic textile substrates, viz., wool, silk and nylon. The effect of various natural and synthetic mordants was studied on the colour uptake and the fastness properties.

With the knowledge that certain natural products, along with colour can give simultaneous desirable properties such as antimicrobial resistance on selected substrates, this aspect was also be studied.

METHODOLOGY

Extraction of Dye

Teak leaves were dried in oven at 105°C for 1 hour. 25 gm of oven dried leaves were then crushed to the least possible form and then added to 500 ml of distilled water in a beaker pH was maintained at 7 (for neutral extraction), 4 using acetic acid (for acidic extraction) and 9 using sodium carbonate (for alkaline extraction). The extraction was done at 100°C for 1 hour. The water was replenished throughout the extraction process to maintain at 500 ml.

The extracted dye was filtered through nylon mesh and then it was strained through nylon cloth in order to remove any suspended particles.

Characterisation of the Inorganic Component of Teak Leaves

For the characterization of the dye, the following parameters were tested using ASTM and TAPPI standards.

Estimation of Colour Yield

The colour yield was estimated on the basis of dry weight as:

$$\text{Yield (\%)} = \frac{\text{Weight of extract (grams)}}{\text{Weight of dried roots (grams)}} \times 100 \qquad \text{...(1)}$$

Moisture Content

Moisture content of raw material was determined according to ASTM D 629-99. The percentage moisture content was calculated as given below:

$$MC = \frac{W - d}{W} \times 100 \qquad \text{...(2)}$$

Where,

w = Weight of raw material in moisture equilibrium state at 20°C and 65% relative humidity

d = Weight of raw material dried at 105°C for 1 hour

Ash Content

TAPPI Standard T-211 m-58 was used for the determination of ash content. Ash content was calculated as follows:

$$\% \text{ Ash} = \frac{[illegible]}{[illegible]} \times 100 \qquad \text{...(3)}$$

Where,
A = Weight of crucible after ashing
B = Weight of empty crucible
W = Initial weight of the sample

Dyeing of Silk, Wool and Nylon with Extracted Dye

The dyeing of silk, wool and nylon was done using dye extracted in all the 4 mediums- aqueous (neutral, acidic and alkaline), and n-hexane. The dyeing was carried out under acidic (pH 4) neutral (pH 7) and alkaline (pH 9) conditions. Fabric pieces measuring 10”×10” were cut. The required MLR (1:80 for silk and 1:30 for wool and nylon)) was taken. 100% dye concentration was taken on v/v bases. Dye liquor was stirred well. The pre-soaked samples were added. After dyeing, the samples were removed, rinsed in running water, soaped in Lissapol N, rinsed again and dried.

Effect of Mordanting Methods on Dyeing of Silk, Wool and Nylon

Pre-Mordanting followed by Post Mordanting

1. Natural mordants used:
   - Alum
   - *Harda*
   - Eucalyptus leaves
   - *Supari*
   - Iron filings and jaggery
   - Pomegranate
   - Tamarind
   - *Amla*
2. Chemical mordants used:
   - Copper sulphate
   - Ferrous sulphate

Pre-mordanting with the above mentioned mordants was carried out for the three substrates. Mordant at 10% owf and MLR 1:80 (for silk and nylon) and 1:30 (for wool) was taken and pre-soaked fabric sample was added. Mordanting was done at 100ºC (for wool and nylon) and 80ºC (for silk) for 20 minutes. Pre-mordanted samples were later dyed with the dye extracted in aqueous mediums- alkaline (pH 9), neutral (pH 7) and acidic (pH 5) followed by post mordanting with the same mordant. After 20 minutes samples were removed, soaped at 50°C for 20 minutes with 0.5 g/l Lissapol N to remove the unfixed dye, and dried at room temperature [11].

Colour Measurement and Fastness Properties

The colour yield (K/S) values with selected mordants were calculated from reflectance measurements using the Kubelka-Munk equation. Colour fastness properties of dyed samples with mordant were evaluated using standard procedures. Wash Fastness of all samples was evaluated using a laundrometer as per the ISO-2 specifications. Light fastness of the dyed samples was determined using the MBTF Light Fastness Tester. For perspiration fastness ISO-2 Standards using perspirometer was followed. Fastness to rubbing of the dyed samples was determined by using a Crockmeter.

The process followed to prepare the printed designs were as follows:

Pre mordanting → **Print with dye** → **Post mordanting**

After application of the mordant by exhaust method, the dye was printed followed by steaming for fixation.

Antibacterial Activity Assessment of Dye and Dyed Textile Materials

1. **Test Organism:** Gram positive (*Staphylococcus aureus*) and Gram Negative Bacteria *(Escherichia coli)*
2. **Culture Medium:** Nutrient agar (for *S.Aureus*) and EMB Agar (for *E.Coli*)
3. **Test Specimen:**
   - Dye solution of aqueous dye extract (neutral pH) prepared at different concentration viz. 1%, 5%, 10% w/v.
   - Dyed fabrics: The textile substrates (wool and silk) control, unmordanted dyed and mordanted with iron filings with jaggery solution and dyed with dye extracted at neutral pH were analysed foe their antimicrobial activity. Rectangular specimens measuring 25 × 50 mm were tested.
   - Instruments used were Incubator and Laminar Flow Chamber.
4. **Test Methods Used:**
   - Qualitative Assessment of the Dye in Solution Form was done by AATCC 30 Method (Disc diffusion method).
   - Qualitative Assessment of the Antimicrobial Activity of the Fabric Samples was done by Parallel Streak Method (AATCC 147).

RESULT AND DISCUSSION

The present study was carried out to systematically explore the feasibility of dyeing silk, wool and nylon with teak leaves. The aim of the study was to extract the dye in different mediums and dye the fabrics with the extracted dye using selected natural and synthetic mordants. The dyed samples were assessed for colour value and fastness to washing, perspiration, rubbing and light. The antimicrobial properties of the selected dyed fabrics were also evaluated.

Extraction of Dye

Dye was extracted from the waste Teak leaves in aqueous medium at varying pH (5, 7 and 9) and in n-hexane. Non-sticky dye residue was obtained on removal of the solvent. Yield % of the dye obtained was determined and results are presented in Table 1.

Table 1: Yield% of Dye Residue Obtained from Teak Leaves by Extraction in Various Mediums

Medium of Extraction	*Yield %*
Aqueous, pH 5	31%
Aqueous, pH 7	28%
Aqueous, pH 9	40%
n-Hexane	1.6%

Characterisation of the Inorganic Component of Teak Leaves

1. *Moisture content:* The leaves were air dried at room temperature and their initial weight was taken. The leaves were oven dried and weight was taken again to calculate the moisture content according to the standard procedure. The moisture content for the teak leaves was found to be 70%.
2. *Ash content:* The ash content for the teak leaves was found to be 8.2%.

Standardisation of Dyeing Method

Dyeing of wool, silk and nylon was carried out with aqueous mediums only for the final sample preparation using acidic, neutral and alkaline extracts. M.L.R. was maintained at 1:30 for wool and 1:80 for silk and nylon. Dyeing was carried out on v/v basis. Temperature of dyeing for wool and nylon was kept at 100°C while for silk it was 80°C.

Effect of pH of Extraction on Colour Value of Unmordanted Fabrics Dyed using Teak Leaves

Wool, silk and nylon were dyed with the dye extracted in aqueous medium at different pH. The colour value and L*,a*,b* values were measured for the dyed samples. Table 2 shows the results for unmordanted dyed wool, silk and nylon.

It was observed that a range of colours, i.e. from pinks to purples to browns could be obtained on unmordanted samples.

It was noted that maximum K/S value was obtained when the unmordanted fabrics were dyed with the dye extracted at pH 5 (acidic) and minimum K/S value is obtained when the unmordanted fabrics were dyed with the dye extracted at pH 7 (neutral).

It was also observed that L* value of the fabric decreased with the decrease in pH of the extract thus indicating that the samples became darker in colour. At the same time, a* value increased with the decrease in pH, thus supporting the fact that the samples became redder. Maximum c* value of the samples dyed with the dye extracted at pH 5 and minimum value of the samples dyed with the dye extracted at pH 9 showed that the fabrics became brighter as the pH of extraction moved from alkaline (9) to acidic (5). Lower b* value of the sample dyed with dye extracted in alkaline medium (pH 9) and neutral medium (pH 7) signifies that the sample hues were more towards blue.

Standardization of Parameters for Application of Selected Mordants

In order to obtain variety of shades and to study the effect of mordants, pre and post mordanting was done with mordants such as alum, *harda,* eucalyptus leaves, *supari,* pomegranate peel, *amla*, tamarind, iron filings with jaggery, ferrous sulphate and copper sulphate. In the premordanting method, mordant application was followed by dyeing with the dye extracted in different pH. Dyeing was followed by a post mordanting treatment with the same mordant (Table 3).

Assessment of Colour Fastness Properties of Dyed Samples

Unmordanted and mordanted wool, silk and nylon fabrics were dyed with aqueous dye extract obtained at neutral, acidic and alkaline pH. These samples were evaluated for their colour fastness properties in terms of light, wash, perspiration and crock/ rub fastness.

Light Fastness

The unmordanted dyed wool and silk had shown light fastness readings in the range of 3/4 - 4/5 which is moderate to good light fastness and for nylon was in the range of 4-8 which is good to excellent. When fabrics were post mordanted after dyeing, the light fastness was found to be improved. This could be because of the complex formation between the mordant and dye which results in the improvement of light fastness. This trend though was not seen for all mordants. When the fabrics are mordanted with *supari,* their light fastness seemed to be reduced. Nylon showed excellent light fastness rating of 7-8 but with some mordants such as *amla* and *supari*, its light fastness reduced slightly.

Wash Fastness

Wash fastness of all the samples was evaluated according to the ISO-2 test method. The samples were qualitatively rated using the standardized grey scale for assessing change in colour and staining.

The result obtained for unmordanted dyed samples showed good to excellent wash fastness for wool, silk and nylon dyed with acidic extract, moderate to very good wash fastness when dyed with aqueous alkaline and neutral extracts.

All samples showed excellent wash fastness rating for staining on white fabric. Even though there was some change in colour from the original samples but the dye which comes out does not seem to be staining the adjacent fabric.

Perspiration Fastness

The dyed samples were tested for their perspiration fastness according to BS 1006. The samples were assessed using the standardized grey scale for change in colour and staining.

It was observed that the unmordanted wool, silk and nylon dyed with acidic extract showed very good perspiration fastness with both acidic and alkaline perspiration solutions while the ones that were dyed with alkaline and neutral extract show fair to good perspiration fastness. Perspiration fastness of samples mordanted with *amla*, tamarind, pomegranate peel, *harda*, iron fillings with jaggery showed very good perspiration fastness but the samples mordanted with alum, *supari*, copper sulphate, ferrous sulphate and eucalyptus leaves showed slightly reduced fastness to perspiration.

Fastness to Rubbing

The rub fastness of unmordanted dyed samples and mordanted dyed samples was tested under dry and wet conditions. In both the cases, most of the samples showed good to excellent fastness results and the ratings were between 4/5 to 5. Results were better for dry rub fastness as compared to wet fastness. Both unmordanted dyed as well as mordanted dyed samples showed excellent dry and wet crock fastness for both colour change and staining.

Assessment of Antimicrobial Activity

Samples were qualitatively assessed for their antimicrobial activity against gram negative bacteria, *E.coli* and gram positive bacteria, *S.aureus*. The extracted dye samples (in powder form) were assessed by disc diffusion method and the dyed samples were assessed by parallel streak method.

Different concentrations of extracted dye were taken viz. 1%, 5% and 10% v/v. There was a complete lack of bacterial growth observed underneath the disk in both *E.coli* and *S.aureus* whereas bacterial growth was observed around the disc wherever bacteria was applied [Plate 1: a, b, c and d]. This indicated that the dye extracted was bactericidal and not bacteriostatic.

The qualitative assessment of the antimicrobial activity against gram negative (*E.coli*) [Plate 2: a, b, c, and d] and gram positive (*S.aureus*) [Plate 3: a, b, c, and d] showed restricted bacterial growth on unmordanted dyed fabric surface as compared to control sample. Whereas, mordanted dyed wool samples showed excellent antimicrobial property against gram negative bacteria (*E.coli*) but there was little microbial growth on the surface of mordanted dyed wool samples in the presence of gram positive bacteria (*S.aureus*).

The results for antimicrobial activity against gram negative (*E.coli*) [Plate 2: a, b, c, and d] and gram positive (*S.aureus*) [Plate 3, a, b, c and d] bacteria for unmordanted dyed and mordanted dyed silk fabric were further assessed. There was some bacterial growth of gram positive as well as gram negative bacteria underneath the unmordanted dyed samples whereas, mordanted samples showed complete lack of growth against both gram positive and gram negative bacteria.

Therefore selected mordants in combination with the dye seemed to further improve the antibacterial activity as hardly any bacterial growth was seen in these samples for silk and wool. The results were slightly better for silk though.

Combination of Dyeing and Printing with Extracted Dye and Selected Mordants

Different combinations of mordants were tried for printing. Samples were pre mordanted using exhaust method, printed with the extracted dye followed by post mordanting by exhaust method.

Table 4 gives the range of shades and prints obtained for various combinations. The samples were washed using ISO-II method and the ratings for both change in colour and staining on white have also been presented in Table 4.

Table 2: K/S and Colour Value of Unmordanted Dyed Textile Substrates

Fabric	*pH of Extraction*	*K/S*	*L**	*a**	*b**	*c**	*h**	*Sample*
Wool	5	4.161	47.70	14.01	9.85	17.13	35.10	
	7	2.793	48.24	11.88	2.73	12.19	12.94	
	9	2.654	51.16	8.14	3.49	8.86	23.21	
Silk	5	2.831	56.67	11.11	14.91	18.59	53.29	
	7	1.938	59.32	10.09	2.13	10.31	11.93	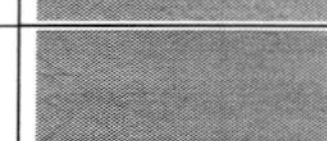
	9	1.668	60.90	9.93	2.05	10.14	11.64	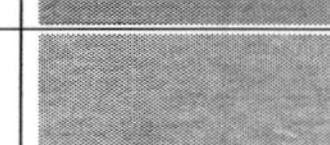
Nylon	5	1.773	25.31	20.36	26.13	33.12	52.06	
	7	2.30	21.40	16.44	03.34	16.78	348.51	
	9	1.410	32.85	12.26	1.57	12.36	352.72	

Table 3: Colour Value of Mordanted Dyed Textile Substrates

Mordant	*pH of Extraction*	*Silk*	*Wool*	*Nylon*
Alum	5			
	7			
	9			

Mordant	*pH of Extraction*	*Silk*	*Wool*	*Nylon*
Harda	5			
	7			
	9			
Amla	5			
	7			
	9			
Iron filings with Jaggery	5			
	7			
	9			
Supari	5			
	7			
	9			
Eucalyptus leaves	5			
	7			
	9			

Mordant	*pH of Extraction*	*Silk*	*Wool*	*Nylon*
Pomegranate peel	5	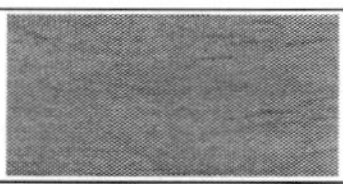	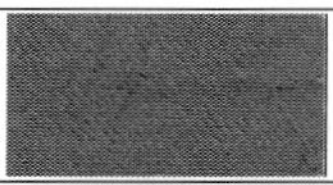	
	7			
	9			
Ferrous Sulphate	5			
	7			
	9			
Copper Sulphate	5			
	7			
	9			
Tamarind	5			
	7			
	9			

Table 4: Combinations of Dyeing and Printing with Selected Mordants and Extracted Dye

Mordant	*Wash Fastness*			*Samples*
	CC	*SC*	*SS*	
Harda	4	5	5	

Mordant	*Wash Fastness*			*Samples*
	CC	*SC*	*SS*	
Pomegranate peel	4	5	5	
Tamarind	5	5	5	
Copper sulphate	5	5	5	
Ferrous sulphate	4/5	5	5	
Supari	4/5	5	5	

Gram negative bacteria (*E.coli*)

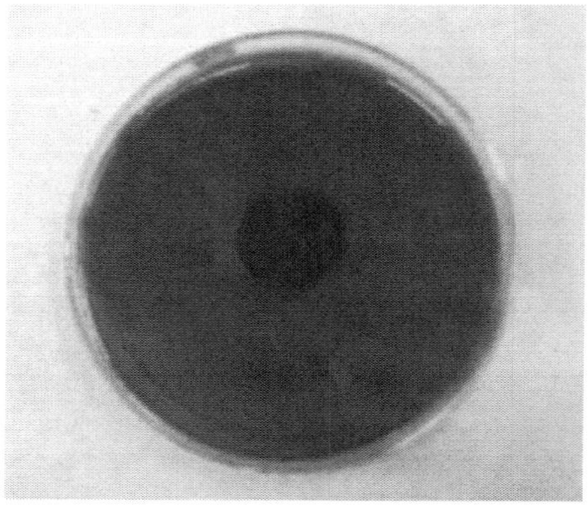

(a) Control

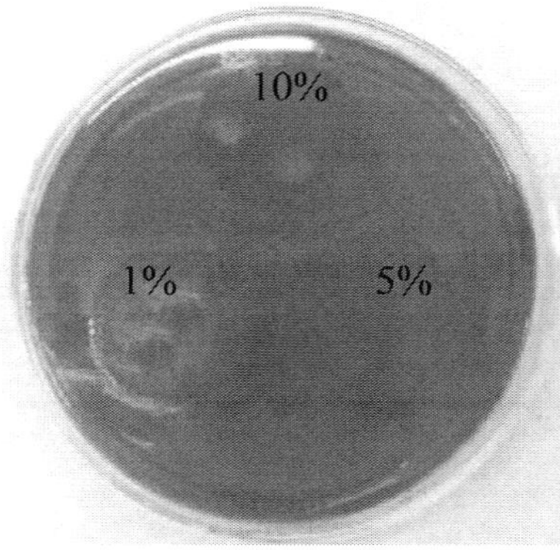

(b) 1%, 5% and 10% Dye

Gram positive bacteria (*S. aureus*)

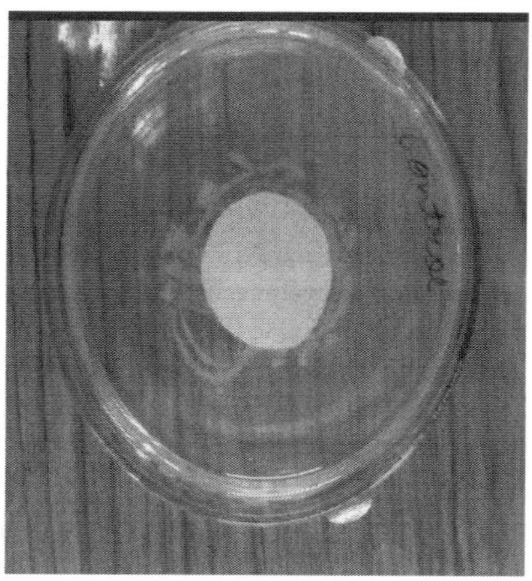

(c) Control

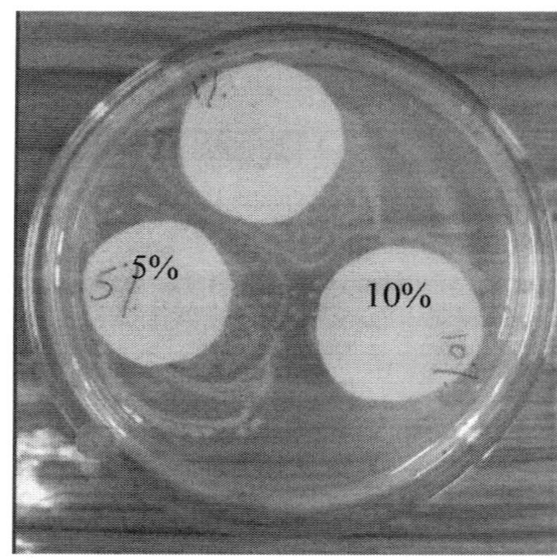

(d) 1%, 5% and 10% Dye

Plate 1: Qualitative Aseeessment of Antimicrobial Activity of Dye Extracted Teak Leaves in Neutral Medium (pH 7)

WOOL

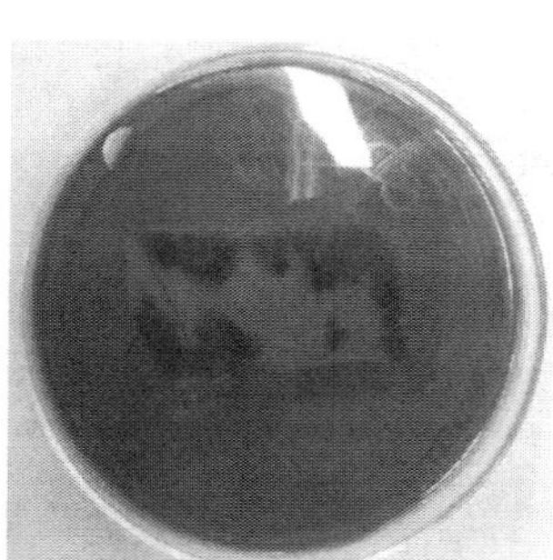

(a) Control

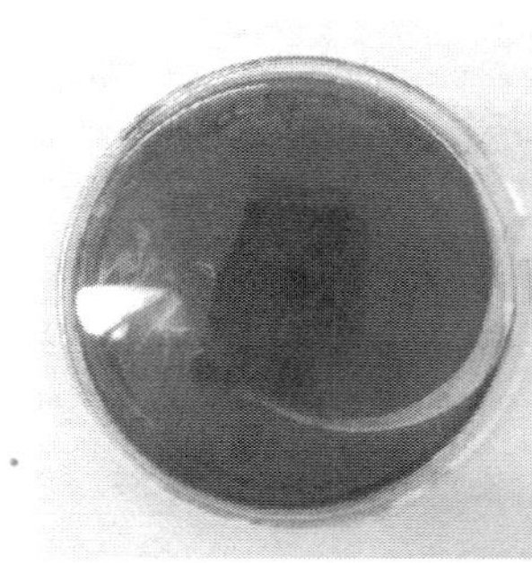

(b) Unmordanted Dyed Wool Fabric

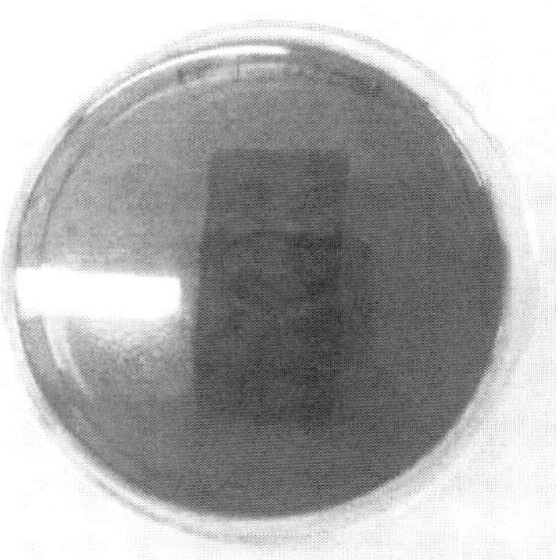

(c) Iron Filings with Jaggery

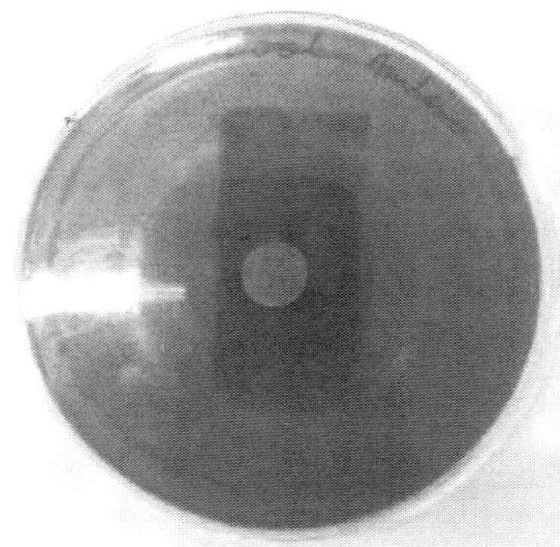

(d) *Amla*

SILK

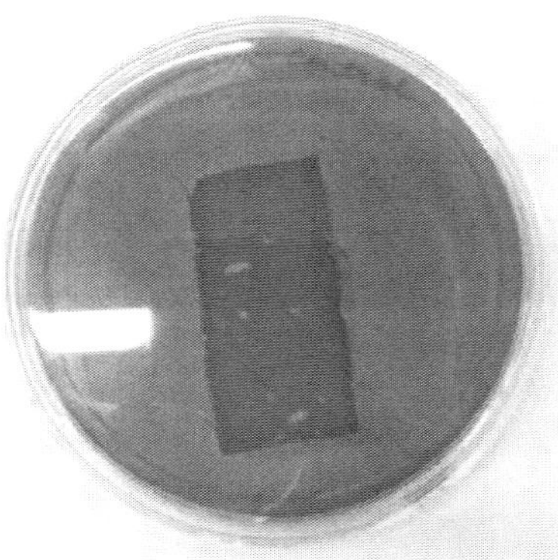

(a) Control

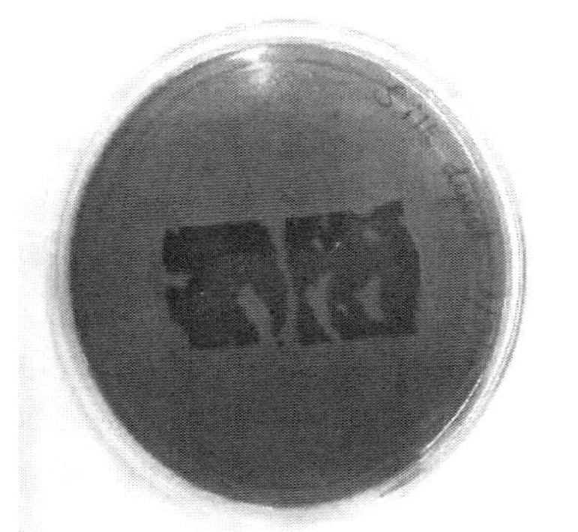

(b) Unmordanted Dyed Silk Fabric

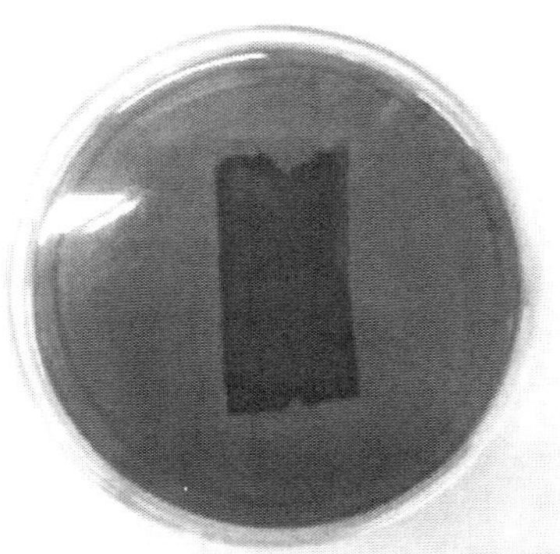

(c) Iron Filings with Jaggery

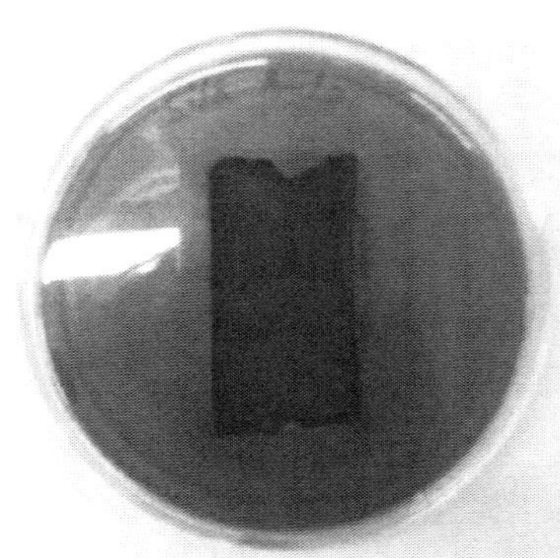

(d) *Amla*

Plate 2: Qualitative Aseeessment of Antimicrobial Activity of Unmordanted Dyed and Mordanted Dyed Wool and Silk Fabrics Dyed with the Dye Extracted from Teak Leaves in Neurral Medium (pH 7) against Gram Negative Bacteria (*E. coli*)

WOOL

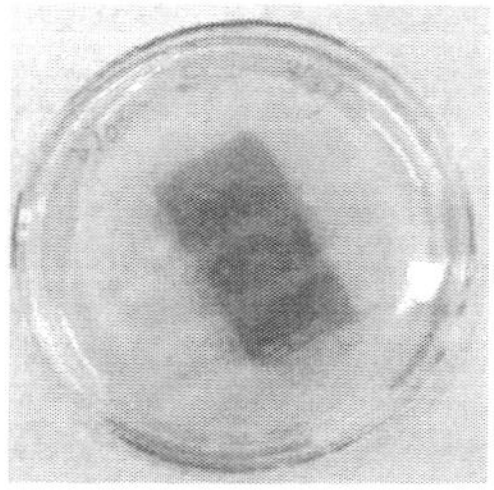

(a) Control

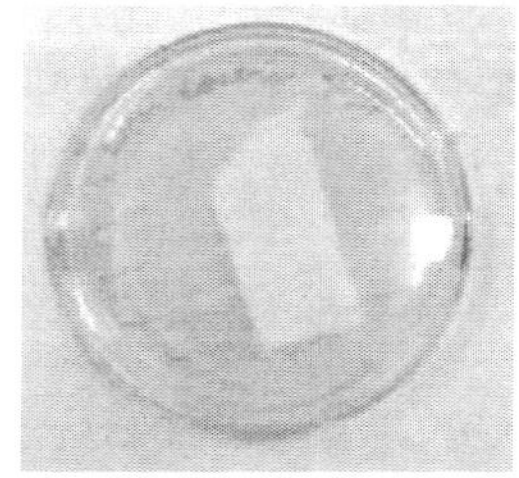

(b) Unmordanted Dyed Wool Fabric

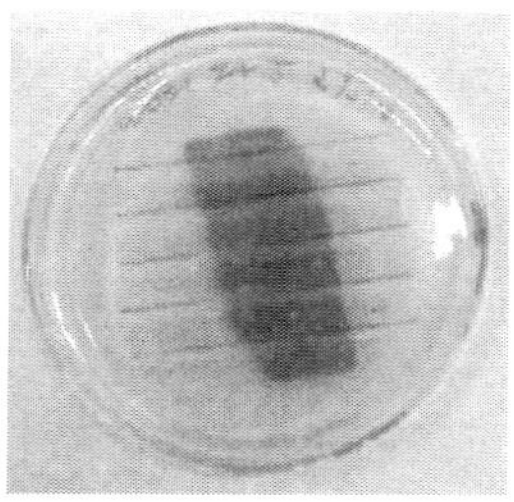

(c) Iron Filings with Jaggery

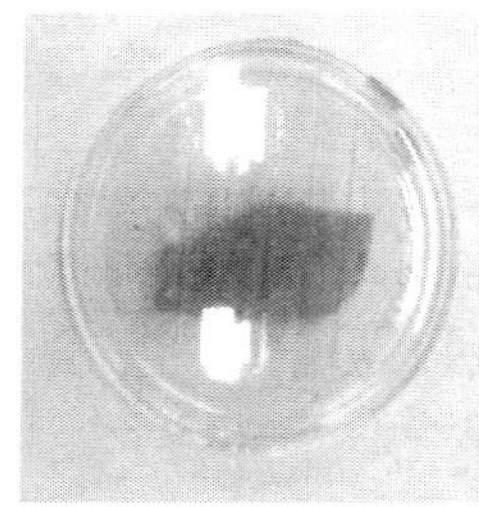

(d) Amla

SILK

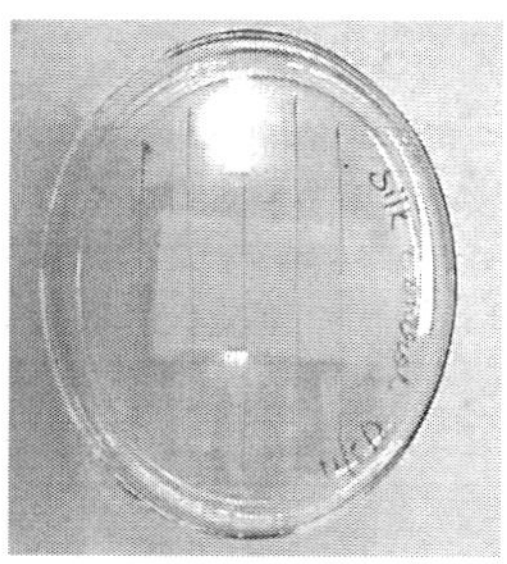

(a) Control

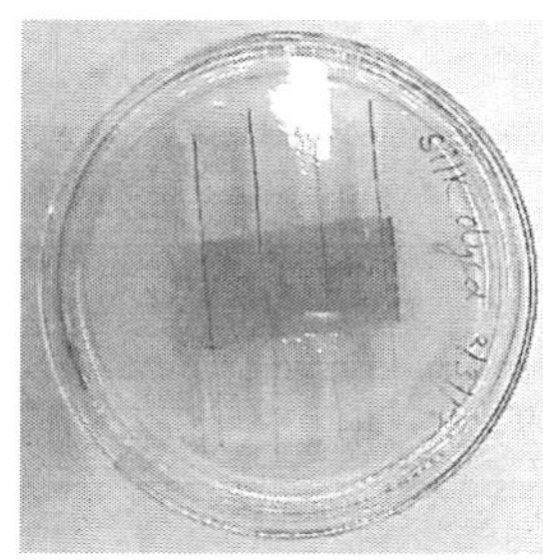

(b) Unmordanted Dyed Silk Fabric

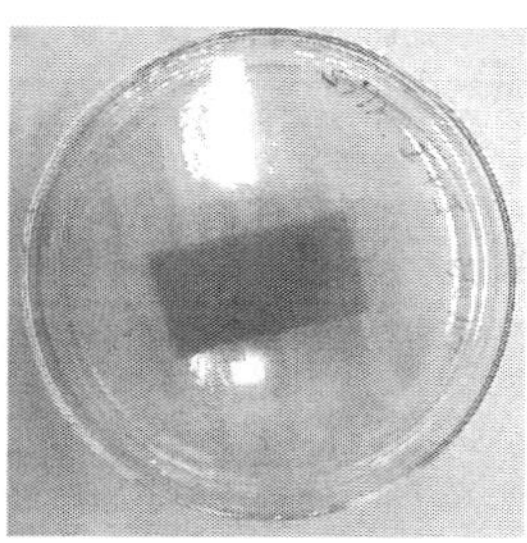

(c) Iron Filing with Jaggery

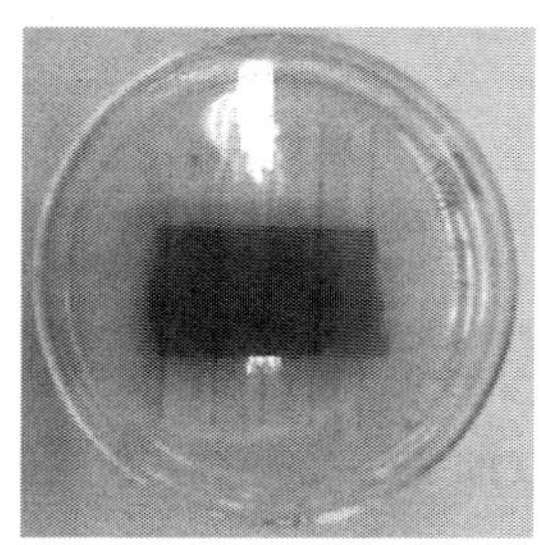

(d) Amla

Plate 3: Qualitative Aseeessment of Antimicrobial Activity of Unmordanted Dyed and Mordanted Dyed Wool and Silk Fabrics Dyed with the Dye Extracted from Teak Leaves in Neutral Medium (pH 7) against Gram Positive Bacteria (*S. aureus*)

CATALOGUE SHOWING DYED AND PRINTED STOLES AND DUPATTAS OF SILK

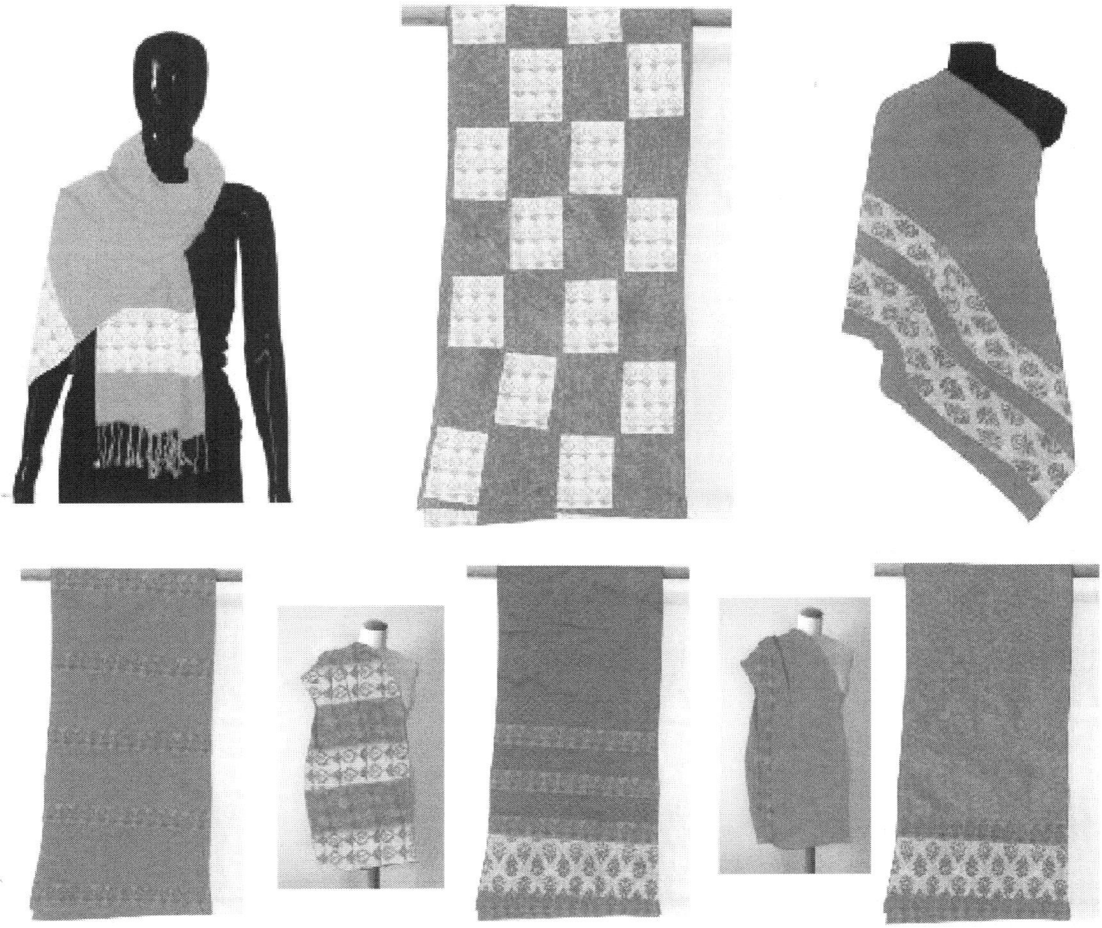

REFERENCES

[1] Bhatia, K., 'Development of Hi-Fashion Cotton Knitwear Using Vegetable Dyes', Unpublished.

[2] Balakumar, C., Kalivani, J., Shivakumar, R. (2011), 'Dyeability and Antimicrobial properties of cotton fabrics finished with *Punica granatum* Extracts', *Journal of Textile and Apparel, Technology and Management*, Vol. 7, Issue 2, pp. 7-8.

[3] Tewari, D.N. (1992), 'A Monograph on Teak (*Tectona grandis*)', Dehra Dun: International Book Distributors.

[4] Aradhana, R., Rao, A.N.V., Chaithanyna, R.K. (2010), 'A Review on *Tectoa grandi. linn*: Chemistry and Medical Uses', Herbal Tech Industry, pp. 6-9.

[5] Bhuyan, R., Saikia, C.N., Das, K.K. (2004), 'Extraction and Identification of Colour Components from the Barks of Mimusops Elengi and Terminalia Arjuna and Evaluations of their Dyeing Characteristic on Wool', *IJFTR*, 29 (12), pp. 470-476.

[6] David and Richardson, S. (2016), 'Asian Textile Studies: Brown Dyes'.

[7] Elvin. T. (1992), Utilization of Tannins in Indonesia, in Plant Polyphenols: Synthesis, Properties, Significance, Hemingway and Laks (eds), New York, pp. 881-894.

[8] Saxena, S., Varadarajan, P.V., and Shaikh, A.J. (2005), 'Dyeing Potential of the Leaves of Emblica Officinalis, Eucalyptus Globulus and *Tectona grandis* for Cotton'.

[9] Tewari, D.N. (1992), 'A Monograph on Teak (*Tectona grandis*)', Dehradun: International Book Distributors.

[10] Widiawati, D. (2009), 'The Revival of the Usage of Natural Fibers and Natural Dyes in Indonesian Textiles', *Journal of Visual Arts and Design* 3, Issue 2, pp. 115–128.

[11] Gulrajani, M.L. (1998), 'Mordant, Natural Dyes and their Application to Textile', Department of Textile Technology, IIT, Delhi.

Process of Bagh Printing in Madhya Pradesh

AMRITA RAJPUT[1] AND JAMNA MISHRA[2]

[1] *HOD Design, Sage University, Indore*

[2] *HOD Journalism, Sage University, Indore*

E-mail: rajput.amrita@gmail.com

ABSTRACT

In traditional hand block printing, Bagh print is one of the famous craft belongs to the state of Madhya Pradesh in India. It represents the rich heritage, unique craft and culture of India. Bagh print is a name given to the craft of hand block printing done in Bagh village of Madhya Pradesh famous for the use of natural color and its vibrant red color is a result of local water specialty. Some 400 years ago hand block printer 'Muslim Khatri' community migrated from Sindh region of today's Pakistan to Manavar in Madhya Pradesh and then finally settled in the Bagh village. Hand block printing is an age-old craft to design the fabric using wooden blocks to print with hands using natural colors on it.

In Bagh printing, motifs are basically inspired from the local flora and fauna found in the region. Motifs inspired from the jasmine flower, mushroom and lehriya pattern are used in printing. A combination of traditional buta and buti designs used in printing are the specialty of Bagh print. Some times jaal inspired from the intrinsic Mughal design pattern is also used in printing. Today geometrical designs also used to keep with the pace of market demand. The late Ismailji Khatri, a master craftsman belonging to the traditional Muslim Khatri community, developed Bagh printing process in the year 1960. He made this craft famous by experimenting on bed sheets and table covers. Before that Bagh print was limited to the tribal market only and used to make tribal wearing known as lugda and lugdi worn by tribal women. To keep the tradition alive, documentation is required and this paper is an attempt to document the process used in Bagh print.

Keywords: *Natural dyes, Art and craft of Madhya Pradesh, Evolution of printing in India, Bagh print process, Hand block printing, Muslim khatri.*

INTRODUCTION

Traditional hand block printing is a very old craft of embellishing fabric using wooden blocks to print on variety of natural fiber based fabrics with natural colors. Documented history of the hand block printing suggests that hand block printed cotton with beautiful motifs were famous during the times of Alexander the great in 327 B.C. and even older than that.

During the excavation of archaeological survey few statues of Mohenjo-Daro times wearing scarf similar to ajrakh hand block printing suggests that hand block printing was in practice some 4000 years ago too. These evidences shows that India was a home of hand block printed textiles since many centuries.

In India since ancient times many hand block printing techniques have been developed and Bagh print is one of such hand block printing technique developed in last 100 years in the Bagh village of Dhar district in Madhya Pradesh.

Bagh: An Introduction

Bagh printing is done in a small village known as Bagh situated one fifty kilometers away from Indore. There is an ancient temple dedicated to the Maa Durga riding tiger known as 'Bagheshwari' temple. A hand block printing done in Bagh is having its peculiarity in its red color due to high copper content in local river water known as 'Baghini'.

Bagh is having a majority of tribal population comprises of various tribes like Bhils, Bhilalas, and other backward castes such as Kurmis, Sirvi and Muslim population. "Khatri" muslims are basically involved in the craft of hand block printing and employs various tribal people as their helpers to perform various related activities. Today there are almost 15 hand block printing units working in the village employing almost 2500 to 3000 people in their work. In the year 2009 Bagh print got geographical indication from government of India.

Bagh Print

A group of 'Muslim Khatri' who were traditional hand block printers migrated from Sindh region of today's Pakistan to Manavar in Madhya Pradesh some 400 years ago in search of new opportunities. Late Ismailji Khatri a master craftsman from Manavar involved in the craft of hand block printing since generations shifted to Bagh in the year 1962 in search of better water facility. Traditional hand block printing process requires flowing water and 'Baghini' river in Bagh was providing ideal condition for it.

Bagh printers were known as alizarin printers before 1980 when for the first time one of the India's famous craft patrons Late Martand Singh gave these alizarin printers from Bagh a name 'Bagh Printers'. Since then alizarin print from Bagh got its name Bagh print. With the changing time, Late Ismailji Khatri experimented with different fabrics and with little changes in the traditional process they developed a unique process to print fabrics as per the modern needs which is today known as Bagh print to the world. Presently all the craftsmen in Bagh following the same process in hand block printing developed by Ismail jiKhatri.

Previously bagh printing was limited to tribal market only. Bagh hand block printing was done on products like lugda, lugdi and turban basically worn by tribal population in the past but it was Late Ismail ji Khatri and his family started exploring new product lines and successfully experimented with bed sheets, table covers and sarees. Today it is even used to print bamboo mats and variety of nature based fibers.

REGIONS OF HAND BLOCK PRINTING IN INDIA

Hand block printing done exclusively in Bagh village is known as Bagh print. However, other states and areas in India famous for block printing are:

Table 1: Hand Block Printing Centers in India

S. No.	*Name of the State*	*Block Printing Center*
1.	Gujarat	Anjar, Ajrakhpur, Dhamadka
2.	Rajasthan	Akola, Bagru, Barmer, Balotara
3.	Andhra Pradesh	Masulipatnam
4.	Tamilnadu	Tanjore
5.	Madhya Pradesh	Bagh, Tarapur

Based on secondary data.

PRODUCER COMMUNITIES

In Bagh, hand block printing work is dominated by 'Muslim Khatri' community. Presently out of 15 units, 12 units of hand block printing are owned by Muslim khatri families. Rest 3 hand block printing units are owned by Teli community. Artisans working in these units belong to the Bhil, Bhilala, Teli, Rajput, Scheduled caste and other backward communities trained by Khatri community in the craft of hand block printing. There is no linkage in between caste and trade in Bagh printing except most of the master craftsman belongs to the traditional hand block printer Muslim Khatri community.

RAW MATERIALS

In Bagh printing, process variety of raw materials required right from wooden blocks to dyes to fabrics and other materials in preparation of fabric printing and dyeing. Bagh printers source all these raw materials from different places.

Table 2: Sourcing of Eaw Materials in Bagh

S. No.	*Raw Material*	*Place of Sourcing*
1.	Wooden blocks	Farakkabad, Pethapur
2.	Alizarin and other dyes	Indore, Udaipur
3.	Fabric	Bhimandi, Maheshwar, Chanderi

Based on primary data

TOOLS USED

Various tools used in Bagh printing process are as follows:

Vegetable Dyes

In Bagh printing process basically two natural colors are used, i.e. red and black. In prepraring black color iron rust fermented with jiggery powder for 15 days to get prepared. For red color alum is used to print on the fabrics as a mordant and then dyed with alizarin and dhawdi flower. Alizarin is one of the rich sources for red color. Base of the fabric is prepared with harad (myrabalan) powder as a source of tannin to absorb and fix natural colors. Black color is printed directly but for red alum water mix with tamarind seed powder to prepare a paste and then dyed with alizarin using boiling process.

Wooden Blocks

Wooden block is one of the most important tool used in Bagh printing. Teakwood is used to make these blocks purchased from Farakkabad in Uttar Pradesh or Pethapur in Gujarat. Pricing of the block depends upon the size, design pattern and labor involved in making blocks but price of a considerably good block starts from Rs. 1000. The carpenters involved in block making since generations prepare these blocks.

Printing Tables

In other block printing centers use of table started to print fabrics but in Bagh still a traditional 'Patia' (very small table) made of wood is used to print the fabrics. Printers print the fabrics in sitting position. This patia or very small table is 4 to 5 feet in length, 1 foot in breadth and 10 inches in height. This very small table is covered with a thick and plain cloth for protection; while used in printing by artisans.

THE PROCESS OF BAGH PRINTING

The process of Bagh printing is as follows.

- **Design preparation:** A master craftsman prepares a design on the plain paper or graph paper varies from the geometrical pattern to flora pattern or can be inspired from a historic monument or temple.
- **Wood selection for block making:** Teakwood is preferred in making blocks because of its long lasting quality and life. Teakwood is chosen without defects in preparing the blocks.
- **Block preparation:** Carpenters uses his tools to smoothen the teakwood and carve as per the design provided by the master craftsman. For exact design carpenter put the graph paper provided by the master craftsman over selected teakwood and start carving using his tools.
- **Design engraving and checking the blocks:** Once the carpenter carves the design using his tools he gives a final finishing touch using different tools. After first carving is done carpenter print it on the plain paper to check the appropriateness of the design. If he finds it ok, then deliver it to the craftsmen if not he will again give the final touch using his carpentry tools and then recheck again. After satisfaction with the result he delivers it to the master craftsman.
- **Block preservation:** When master craftsman received the block he will check it by printing on the plain cloth and if finds it suitable for printing, then he will put the block in oil for 2 to 3 days. This process helps master craftsman to protect wooden block from insects and also increase the strength of the wood. This also helps to protect block from water used in preparing paste for printing.
- **Fabric preparation for printing:** For traditional hand block printing in Bagh, nature based fiber clothes used for printing. Master craftsmen source raw fabric from various dealers in Bhiwandi (Maharashtra), Chanderi and Maheshwar. After procuring the fabric it goes through various stages such as:

  First raw fabric is put in a solution made from soda ash, goat dung, sea salt and castor oil for 24 hours. After 24 hours fabric is washed with clean water and then put in sunlight for drying, it also works as a natural bleaching. In this process immense heat is produced which makes the fiber absorbent and soft. After repetition of this step 2 to 3 times fabric put it in a solution of harada (myrabalan) and then put it in sunlight so that fabric becomes yellow. The logic behind fabric dipping into harada solution is to make fabric tannin rich to absorb the natural color and when printing with iron rust and jiggery powder solution it becomes black. Now the fabric is ready for printing.

- **Printing of clothes:** Two different pastes made to get red and black color in printing. To get black iron rust and jiggery powder mix with water kept in an iron or plastic vessel for 15 days to get it prepared. For red first alum is mix with water to prepare alum water. After this a paste made from tamarind seed powder is used. Now yellowish fabric is put on the table for block printing with the desired design.

  After this preparation is done if craftsman wants to print black he will mix iron rust and jiggery powder solution in tamarind seed powder paste and put it in a wooden tray and start printing. For red alum water is mix with tamarind powder paste again and put it in wooden tray and starts printing.
- **Drying:** After printing is done, the fabric is put on the stones to dry it in the sunlight. Then the printed fabric is kept in a dry place for 4 to 5 days so that fabric absorbs the natural color well. After this 'vichlai' process is performed. In this process fabric is washed in running water probably in river so that all the extra color gets washed away from the fabric. Then fabric is put in sunlight for drying. The fabric is ready for dyeing.
- **Dyeing process:** In first dyeing process which is known as 'Bhatti' or boiling process fabric is dyed with alizarin and dhawadi flower. In this process, black color is fixed and in place of alum printing red comes out due to alizarin. In this alizarin dyeing process, a copper vessel is used which helps to get better color than any other metal. After this alizarin dyeing process is over fabric is again put in sunlight to get dry. After drying if it does need to dye with other natural colors like turmeric for yellow, pomegranate rind for deep yellow, tesu (bastard teak) flower for orange is used. If it does not required to be dyed again, then it undergoes bleaching process for cleansing of spots on the fabric
- **Finishing:** Once fabric is bleached and dried in sunlight, it goes for ironing and is ready to market.

FINAL PRODUCTS FOR MARKET

Mainly Bagh printers produce sarees, stoles, salwar suit and bed cover. Sometimes they also print wall hangings as per the customer demands.

REFERENCES

[1] Tahir, A. (2013), Bagh Print a Global Brand, *Madhya Pradesh Sandesh*, 55-56.

[2] Bhagavatula, S. (2010), The Working of Entrepreneurs in a Competitive Low Technology Industry: The Case of Master Weavers in the Handloom Industry, http://ssrn.com/abstract=2122434,

[3] Chakraborty, K.S. (2006), *Entrepreneurship and Small Business Development*, New Delhi, Mittal Publication, pp. 47-57.

[4] Charantimath, P. (2009), *Entrepreneurship Development Small Business Enterprises*, New Delhi, Pearson Education.

[5] Dwivedi, A.K. and Sukhwal, A. (2012), *Rural Entrepreneurship Development in Liberalized Era*, New Delhi, Bookwell Publication, pp. 257-271.

[6] Emmaniel, R. (2012), A Profile of Handloom Industry in India, *Journal of Exclusive Management Science*, 1(7).

[7] Fillis, I. (2002), The Entrepreneurial Artist as Marketer, *The New Wave: Entrepreneurship & the Arts*, Melbourne, Australia.

[8] Jain, R. and Goswami, R. (2010), Livelihood through Handloom Weaving, *International Research Journal*, pp. 1-3.

[9] Kumar, P., Sultana, M.S. and Pillaii, M.K. (2010), Strategies to Improve Sales of Handloom Products with Special Reference to Pauducherry, *TECHNIA Journal of Management Studies*, 2010, pp. 16-26.

[10] Kumudha, A. and Rizwana, M. (2013), Problems Faced by Handloom Industry – A Study with Handloom Weavers' Co-operative Societies in Erode District, *International Journal of Management and Development Studies*, pp. 50-56.

[11] Markelow, G. and Bill, M. (2001), Towards a Model of Entrepreneurial Marketing for Rural Women: A Case Study Approach, *Journal of Developmental Entrepreneurship*, pp. 221-235.

[12] Narzary, J. (2013), Marketing Problems and Prospects of Handloom and Handicrafts Industry in B.T.A.D., *Global Research Methodology*, pp. 1-8.

[13] Joshi, P., Singh A.B. and Saxena, M. (2014), Success through Entrepreneurial Marketing of Rural Handicraft: Cases of Ajrakh Print and Bagh Print, *Asian Journal of Research in Social Sciences and Humanities*, pp. 147-156.

[14] Samiruddin, M. Rahman, A. Saxena and H. Dwivedi (2004), *Rural Marketing Thrust and Challenges*, Jaipur, National Publishing House, pp. 281-286.

Minimizing Waste Generation: Role of the Designer

ANANYA MITRA PRAMANIK[1] AND ANJALI AGRAWAL[2]

[1] *Research Scholar, School of Fashion and Design, G D Goenka University, Gurgaon, Haryana*
Assistant Professor, National Institute of Fashion Technology, New Delhi
[2] *Assistant Professor, School of Fashion and Design, G D Goenka University Gurgaon, Haryana*
E-mail: ananya.pramanik@nift.ac.in; anjali.agrawal@gdgoenka.ac.in

ABSTRACT

This paper affirms the role of design as an important tool for influencing the world and minimising waste. It evaluates the contribution of an ethical designer to combat waste generation and to ensure sustainable growth for the future generations.The design industry is ever changing according to consumer demands and trends. "Within a consumer oriented society, the job of the designer is to make products and services more appealing," thus design today is moving away from aesthetics to commerce. It is also focusing more on sales volume and less on ethics and social responsibility. There is an immediate need of the designer to transform this trend and work along ethical values. A designer is the link between the consumer and the manufacturer. It is in his domain to influence sustainable manufacturing as well as make the consumer aware of the dangerous trend of fast fashion and its impact on the environment.

Keywords: *Consumerism, Ethics, Designer, Waste, Sustainable.*

INTRODUCTION

The demands of the fashion industry keep changing from season to season. There is a quick variation in requirements and the garments produced have a short life span. The products are discarded before they are worn out due to the changes in the fashion dictates. This phenomenon is known as 'fast fashion'.[1] As a result of mass production, fast fashion products are easily available at a cheap cost. This leads to rapid rejection of fabrics and generates huge amount of fabric waste. Sometimes this waste gets recycled but much of the volume of clothing often ends up in landfills (Figure 1). This large volume of textile waste is not sustainable even if the fabrics are bio-degradable. The mass production of fabrics leads not only to natural resource depletion but also to pollution for the land, water and air.

Figure 1: Clothing Ending Up in Landfill

Textile manufacturing requires a large number of processes for the creation of various finished fabrics. Most of these processes lead to hazardous waste for land, water and air.[2] Textile mills generate 1/5th of the world's industrial water pollution. It uses around 20,000 chemicals, many of them are carcinogenic and destroys our ecosystem.[3]

Textiles are also the fastest growing sector in household waste.[4] It can be categorised into two types:

1. *Pre-manufacturing textile waste:* Pre-manufacturing textile waste comprises of the litter produced by the processes of growing, manufacturing and extraction of textile fibres. The processing of fabrics including washing, bleaching, combing, carding, sizing, weaving, dyeing, printing etc. Each of these stages requires vast amounts of water, fuel & chemicals. This leads to water pollution, air pollution and energy depletion.
2. *Post manufacturing textile waste:* Post manufacturing textile waste can be of two types:
   (a) Pre-Consumer Waste which comprises of fabrics left over after the textile yardage is shaped into products, selvages and warp yarns wasted while the fabric is being produced, etc.
   (b) Post-consumer wastes which constitutes textile products which are discarded or rejected after use. These include household waste.

Designers should work towards minimizing post-consumer waste or minimizing the creation of this waste, which leads to the damage of our ecosystem. This is called the ethical way of working. '*Ethics*' can be defined as the moral standards against which behavior is judged. Ethics address questions about morality – concepts such as Right and Wrong, Good and Evil, Justice, Virtue etc. Ethics are the standards governing the conduct of an individual, a group or an organization.

Ethical designing involves designing a product; keeping in mind the effects that product is going to have on the society and the environment. Apart from that the best method of minimising waste is to not create waste at all as it is well known that *prevention is better than cure*. Ethical designing involves working towards what is good for our environment and the people. It is the job of the ethical designer to make the consumers conscious of the effects of 'fast fashion ' and consumerism on the environment. If the people are made aware then they will buy expensive, good quality clothing which they will not discard quickly instead of buying cheap quality goods available at a lower cost. The people will be conscious that expensive and good quality clothing hires labourers for a longer period of time on the same clothing so that the quality of garment produced is superior and also the wages of the labourers are not deducted. Once the general people are made aware of this ethical fact then they will refrain from buying a large number of cheap goods and then discarding them fast. The ethical designer must ensure that he/she is not promoting consumerism through their work.

Designers should include in their job the role of making the consumers aware of the dangers of over consumption and waste generation through quick disposal of textile products. Design is a potent instrument for influencing the people and minimise waste generation. An ethical designer can control waste generation and warrant wealth and health of the future generations.The design industry is constantly changing along with the changing culture, trends, knowledge, and the economy. A designer's job is focusing more on sales and on business development. However a designer must focus not only on selling designs but also on ethical issues. This means that the designer must be aware of the consequences of his/her work and its effect on the consumer and the environment. The designer should work towards sustainable development through continuous and deliberate efforts.

THE ETHICAL DESIGNER

Within a consumer oriented society, the job of the designer is mainly to make products and services attractive so that they are consumed quickly.

Thus design today is moving from art to business, focusing more on advertising and corporate clients and less on ethics and social responsibility.[6] Design has a deep influence on people's life. It can be seen in the form of sponsored newspaper articles, corporate logos, packaging, television, web sites, and advertisements through various media. Advertisement set the mood of the mental atmosphere and through them the designers instill the creation of need into the minds of the consumer (Figure 2). In other words a 'need' and a 'desire' are created by the designers inside the minds of the consumer. They create the 'envy' and 'yearning' that fuels the economy.

Figure 2: A Parody Advertisement by Culture Jammers [7]

Advertising affects how people identify a product or company, their beliefs about environmental issues, their way of living, and what they purchase. Designers not only have an important role in the society but also an ethical responsibility towards society. One role of designers is that of communicators or mediators between the manufacturing company and the public. By depicting a message to an audience, they connect a company to its consumers. An ethical designer must keep in mind that a message can be perceived in different ways by different people. The designer should scrutinize the effects of their work before it reaches the public, and also examine the objectives of their client or business employer. If these are not considered at the onset of the design process, then it could be misleading, dishonest, or dangerous for the consumers and the environment. The designers work is often mass produced. The message conveyed gets repeated that many times and has a potential for disaster.

Many designers believe that design is just a job and ethical issues should not be their concern or priority. They have chosen to overlook, the issues that surround the industry. However, many others are bringing the issues to light and truly making a difference, making social and ethical design their life's achievements. Tibor Kalman, an American graphic designer said in 1997, 'I began to worry about what we designers, who are very skillful and have powerful tools at our disposal, are doing in the world – what role we are playing – making the filthy oil company look "clean", making the car brochure higher quality than the car.... Is all that okay, or just the level to which design and many other professions have sunk?'

In 2001, the Graphic Designers Association of Canada adopted a code of ethics and professional conduct. This code establishes a strict set of guidelines and responsibilities for designers towards their clients as well as to the environment, society, and human rights.[8] The code is a courageous movement towards ethics as it establishes that designers have a very prominent responsibility in society. It also suggests that designers should refuse to work for clients that engage in unethical practices, including doing environmental harm or disregarding human rights.

ISSUES SURROUNDING DESIGN

Business houses are dominating most of the power houses of the world. These business houses are rich and powerful. They can manipulate decision making of Governments and policy makers [6]. These also often control the mass media. By offering jobs, manufacturing goods and services these corporations send misleading "feel good" messages to the public which help them in selling their products and growing their businesses. Big and small business houses are instrumental in driving the world towards consumerism for their own growth and development and often at the cost of the environment (6).

Design's role in consumer society is a growing one. As the creators of advertisements, brands, and other portrayals of companies, designers are partially responsible for the wide scale commercialization their clients spread. With constant consumption comes the creation of waste and pollution. The earth simply can't keep up with our greed anymore. Everything from fueling our cars to producing everyday products poisons the earth and threatens our future as a species. Corporations are largely to blame for our over-consumption and its effects.

The main ethical issues that concerns a designer are:

- Ecology
- Sustainability
- Fair trade

- Child labor
- Out workers
- Copyright
- Design communication
- Corporate social responsibility
- Ethical standards in everyday design practice.

The designer must understand the implications of each of these issues and work towards the benefit of mankind at large. One way to design ethically could be by serving a social purpose, or by fulfilling a need in society. Design can be used to open people's eyes to important issues, bring people together for a common purpose, or serve public needs. Political posters, promotions for social events, non-profit organizations, and educational materials for ethical awareness can be practiced.

Another way of designing ethically is by ensuring that business clients are aware of the ethical issues and are willing to make a change for the better. Figure 3 shows the wheel diagram to help designers tackle ethical issues. Efforts must be made by the designer to make his/her client aware of the ethical issues. Researching a client's background is important in keeping personal integrity and to make sure that their work won't be used to represent values, that the designer don't agree with.

A designer must always keep the six Rs in mind while designing, i.e.

- Recycle
- Reuse
- Reduce
- Refuse
- Repurpose
- Repair

Recycling refers to breaking down of textile parts and making new products from the parts that are still useful. Recycling may involve processes like pulling apart jumpers and making the fibres' into new threads and garments.

Reusing is when clothes are given to charities so that they can be worn by new owners.

Reduce waste by eliminating packaging, production steps, and toxic emissions.

Refuse harmful chemicals

Repurposing is using textile items into new ways, e.g. cutting up of old shirts to make patchwork quilts.

Repair the materials to add life to them instead of discarding them. This way less waste gets deposited in the landfills.

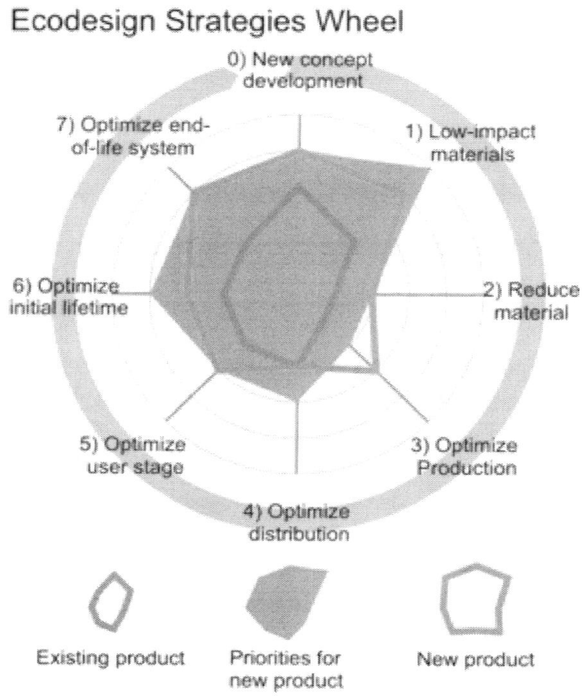

Figure 3: Ecodesign Wheel Diagram to Help Designers Tackle Ethical Issues

Choosing ethically inclined clients may not be possible for many designers and smaller firms, in which case they must be willing to work on a mixture of commercial and ethical engagements whenever it's feasible. They must also use their influential power to push clients into ethical directions. Designers can bring up issues that concern their clients and alert them to the effects they have on society. They can work towards representing the client honestly and fairly. If the business houses are made aware then they can implement ethical measures at a large scale, which benefits both the company and the common people.[6] Fortunately many business houses are becoming aware of the negative effects of over commercialization and willing to work on ethical lines.

CASE STUDY ON MARKS AND SPENCER

Marks and Spencer (M&S), UK is a leading retailer of clothing, foods and home ware in UK. The company operates in about 54 countries worldwide with UK as its primary market.[11] It is headquartered in London, UK and employs about 75,000 people. The company recorded revenues of £9,022 million (approximately $18,113 million) during the financial year (FY) ended March 2008, an increase of 5.1% over 2007.

M&S has Commitments in five areas:

(a) Climate Change:
- To reduce energy consumption.
- To use renewable energy e.g. solar energy and biomass (energy produced from waste from food halls, farms, and factories).
- To use 50% biodiesel for transport.
- Opening of recourse conserving factory with green suppliers.
- To reduce carbon footprint.
- To educate customers in ways to reduce energy consumption and develop low carbon products.

(b) Raw materials
- The source of the raw materials should be certified as sustainable in order to protect the environment.
- Instead of using natural materials alternative materials i.e. made from recycled plastic should be given preference.
- To increase organic farming production.
- To consciously try to reduce usage of water during the manufacturing and production of materials.

(c) Waste:
- To reduce packaging materials by 25%.
- To be carbon neutral by eliminating waste.
- To convert the waste generated into energy.
- Packaging materials should be deliberately created using recycled materials.
- Packaging materials should be bio-degradable.
- Minimize the use of carrier bags.
- To not allow the company's waste to reach the landfill.

(d) Ethical Trading
- Rethink the existing standards in ethical trading.
- Managing labour directly in supply chain.
- Converting existing clothing range to fair cotton trade.
- Educating suppliers to implement best practices in production.
- Helping the special groups, e.g. the disabled to get jobs.

(e) Healthy Eating

- Making the consumers and employees aware of the benefits of a healthy life style
- Aim to increase nutritious foods in the workplace.
- Replacing artificial and fast foods with natural foodstuffs.
- Encouraging the employees to live a healthy life style by providing information and regular health check-ups.[11]

Thus it is clear that with the joint working and understanding of the designers and the business houses ethical concerns can be effectively incorporated in the design practices. This has a long term benefit for the designer, business house as well as the ecology.

CONCLUSION

Design plays a big role in consumerism, globalization, branding, and the un-sustainability of culture. Designers should work towards minimizing this waste or minimizing the creation of this waste, which leads to the damage of our ecosystem. This is called the ethical way of working. The designer should avoid or minimise usage of non-renewable resources so as to impact the environment minimally. Solar, biomass and wind energy are earth friendly alternative energy sources which can be used instead of the conventional energy provided by the fossil fuels. Coal, oil and natural gases are examples of fossil fuels which are not only non renewable but also burning them produces CO_2 gas, which leads to harmful consequences for the earth.

Designers should remember that the most effective way to address waste disposal is by generating less waste and encourage people to relate with the natural environment. Raw materials for design should be carefully chosen. They should be durable and bio degradable. Emphasis should be on the six R's of ethical design i.e. recycle, reuse, reduce, refuse, repurpose and repair. Special efforts should be made for water conservation and preservation. Fabric processing requires a lot of water and water can be saved if processes are combined. Polluted water should be purified before releasing it into the sewage. This will prevent the marine life to be saved from pollution. Codes of design ethics adopted by certain organizations and business houses have significant impact because they open the eyes of designers and challenge them to adopt a view that design should be used for good and avoid all things unethical. Designers who fail to uphold the code risk losing their status as Registered Designers.

The ethical philosophy can be applied in the fields of architecture, landscape architecture, urban design, urban planning, engineering, graphic design, industrial design, interior design, textile and fashion design. It is time designers become aware and examine their role in the world. As talented, creative people, designers have the potential to make very poignant statements that can have positive effects on society.

REFERENCES

[1] Fletcher, K. and Gorse, L. (2012), Fashion & Sustainability: Design for Change. *Fashion & Sustainability: Design for Change.* London: Laurence King Publishing Limited, pp. 124-129.

[2] Parvathi, C., Maruthavanan, T. & Prakash, C. (2009), Environmental Impacts of Textile Industries, http://www.indiantextilejournal.com/; http://www.indiantextilejournal.com/articles/FAdetails.asp?id=2420%20.

[3] Natural Resourse Defence Council (2017), https://www.nrdc.org/issues/encourage-textile-manufacturers-reduce-pollution.

[4] Sinha P., Dissanayake G., Mahwera D., Kahabi C. (2012), Creating a Global Vision for Sustainable Fashion. *Pakistan Textile Journal*, http://www.ptj.com.pk/Web-2012/01-2012/January-2012-PDF/Apparel-and-Knitwear-Recycled-Clothes.pdf

[5] Bairagi, N. (2014), *Journal of Textile Science & Engineering*, omicsgroup.org., http://www.omicsgroup.org/journals/recycling-of-textiles-in-india-2165-8064.S2-003.php?aid=26503

[6] Prusynski, M. (2003), Ethics in Design, http://meganpru.com/oldsite/docs/ethics.pdf

[7] PennState, *http://sites.psu.edu* (2017), The Pennsylvania State University, http://sites.psu.edu/comm411spring2015/2015/02/17/culture-jamming-2/

[8] Code of Ethics and Professional Conduct for Graphic Designers, *www.id2.ca*, https://www.id2.ca/downloads/gdc-ethics.pdf

[9] East Asia Forum. Talking Trash in India (2016), *economywatch.com.* http://www.economywatch.com/features/Talking-Trash-in-India0502.html.

[10] Conceptual Life Cycle Thinking, *www.solidworks.com* (2017), Dassault Systèmes Solid Works Corporation, http://www.solidworks.com/sustainability/sustainable-design-guide/ch4-conceptual-life-cycle-thinking.htm.

[11] Marks & Spencer (2018), *wikipedia.org*, Wikimedia Foundation, Inc., https://en.wikipedia.org/wiki/Marks_%26_Spencer.

[12] Marks and Spencer (2017), http://corporate.marksandspencer.com; http://corporate.marksandspencer.com/media/press-releases/archive/2007/15012007_marksspencer launchesplana200mecoplan.

[13] J., McLennan F. (2004), The Philosophy of Sustainable Design: The Future of Architecture, *The Philosophy of Sustainable Design: The Future of Architecture.* 1st. Missouri: Eco Tone Publishing Company.

[14] Keane, J.D. and Willem te Velde (2008), The Role of Textile and Clothing Industries in Growth and Development Strategies, *www.odi.org.* https://www.odi.org/sites/odi.org.uk/files/odi-assets/publications-opinion-files/3361.pdf

[15] Hawley, J.M. (2004), Textile Recyling: A System Perspective, *http://citeseerx.ist.psu.edu.* Kansas State University, 2004, http://citeseerx.ist.psu.edu/viewdoc/download?doi=10.1.1.563.9556&rep=rep1&type=pdf

[16] Chapman, J. (2016), To Beat the 'Throwaway' Waste Crisis, We Must Design Loveable Objects – That Last, *theconversation.com*, The Conversation Media Group Ltd, 8 March 2016, https://theconversation.com/to-beat-the-throwaway-waste-crisis-we-must-design-loveable-objects-that-last-55269

[17] Sinha, P., Tipi, N.S., Day, C.L., Domvolgou, D. and Beverley, Katharine J. (2015), Supply Chain Challenges for Sustainability: The Case of Waste. *eprints.hud.ac.uk*, http://eprints.hud.ac.uk/id/eprint/24663/1/TipiSupply.pdf

[18] Y., Wang (2006), Recycling in Textiles, *Recycling in Textiles,* 1st, S.l.: Woodhead Publishing.

[19] Fiber to Fashion (2017), Managing Textile Waste, http://www.fibre2fashion.com/industry-article/7267/managing-textile-waste

[20] From a Linear to a Circular Economy (2017), *www.government.nl,* https://www.government.nl/topics/circular-economy/from-a-linear-to-a-circular-economy

[21] Hill, J. Shaw, B. and Hislop, H. (2006), A Zero Waste UK. *Institute for Public Policy Research and Green Alliance,* IPPR and Green Alliance, http://www.green-alliance.org.uk/resources/A%20zero%20waste%20UK.pdf

[22] Norris, L. (2010), *Recycling Indian Clothing* [ed.] Foster J. Indiana: Indiana University Press, pp. 168-169, ISBN 9780253222084.

[23] From Somewhere (2016), *Gather & See,* Gather & See, https://www.gatherandsee.com/designers/from-somewhere/

[24] From Somewhere. *From Somewhere*, http://blog.fromsomewhere.co.uk/

[25] Junky Styling (2016), *www.vam.ac.uk.* Victoria and Albert Museum, http://www.vam.ac.uk/content/articles/j/junky-styling/

Progression towards Green Fashion: An Analysis of High Street Apparel Fabric Composition

ARSHIYA KAPOOR
Assistant Professor, Fashion Design, MIT Institute of Design, Pune
E-mail: arshiyakapoor@mitid.edu.in

ABSTRACT

The fashion industry is buzzing with the words – Sustainable, Eco-friendly, Organic and Carbon footprints. There have been several methods that are applied and many theories are being tested to create and sustain the meagre natural resources that are left on our Planet. There has been a constant dispute on being an Industrial Economy and loosing focus of Green economy. Designing and Production for the new 'Green' Materials and endeavour to find most sustainable route continues.

The most common raw material that is being used for any textile and garment manufacture is Cotton and Polyester. Both make use of the scarce natural resources, in case of Cotton is the huge land mass, water and chemicals that are used during the production and finishing whereas Polyester uses petroleum. The COST comparison of using a recycled raw material as opposed to a virgin material does not fit the tight price points sought by consumers. There has to be a balanced proposition which finds contented Designers, Manufacturers, Retailers and Consumers. Creating a clear road map and creative design ability can bring about significant changes.

The paper attempts to relook at the processes and practices being adopted by leading high street retailers globally. Research will be focussed to analyse if the Mass fashion industry ready to accept raw material that can degenerate/decompose?

Green Economy requires a larger scope and application. Is there a technology or process that can create products – DIFFERENTLY? Products manufactured using raw materials that have minimal effect on natural resources, techniques that have minimum wastage. 'Present' requires making use of the best practices in designing to create awareness that is not just at surface level but also penetrates from thought process to the stores. Design, Production and Retail should be such that they facilitate sustainability.

Keywords: *Fashion design development, High street market, High street brands, Raw material analysis, Green economy, Industrial economy.*

INTRODUCTION

Green Fashion is synonymous with the word Sustainable Fashion. Sustainable is further defined as able to be maintained at a certain rate or level, conserving an ecological balance by avoiding depletion of natural resources, able to be upheld or defended. Being Green and Eco-sensitive has been a priority and focus for most of the leading brands globally.

Today the dominant market is fast paced focusing on mass manufacturing and selling at competitive price. The scenario resembles the consumption pattern of a fast food joint. Wal-Mart, Target, Primark are leading examples of how hypermarkets have changed the way people shop and wear clothes! No one minds buying a $ 6 tank top for a party and then discard it, once it has served its purpose. The quantities in terms of number of garments that are discarded each season have not even lived for 30% of their life.

We can see the huge influence it has had on global market and visible effect in India too. The sharp rise in the Hypermarkets segment within last 5 years gives a clearer picture. The top sellers Big Bazaar, Reliance trends, D-Mart, Hyper city etc. have brought about a massive change in the buying habits. It is further encouraged by big players entering the retail scenario through Amazon, Myntra and Snapdeal. As it is globally pronounced that the Indian market is an 'EMERGING MARKET'. It still has time to reach its peak. Fashion brands across the globe are venturing to capture space in this ever growing market. High street retailers like M&S, H&M, Zara, Promod, GAP to name a few have already set a strong foot in India.

The 'competitive economics', as Wendell Berry writes – fuels adoption of technologies and practices that push both people and natural resources beyond tolerable thresholds

The high street and hypermarkets have increased the number of collections that are put forward each season. The retailers focus on impulse purchasing and each season have a new 'must have piece and look'. This phenomenon is bombarding the consumer with so many clothing options that there is no emotional connect between the user and the garment purchased. To demonstrate this further one can see connect that earlier generation had, especially with each garment piece having a beautiful story to tell.

This paper for the author is not just a theory presentation but also introspection. It is looking within and questioning the preparation and progression to a lifestyle that supports the consumption pattern that will work towards sustainability.

The aim of this paper is to investigate the prominent raw material for high street clothing brands globally. Raw material plays the most vital role, contributing to 60% of the cost for the manufacturer. The choice of material for a product has a major impact on sustainability. Small steps with understanding of a better consumption pattern may hold the key to make thoughtful and smart choice.

LITERATURE REVIEW

Resource and Environmental Profile Analysis: Cotton

Cotton presumably comes across as the most natural choice for fashion. There are several factors that are now cropping up and voicing the huge impact that cotton has on the environmental resources. Land and water the most critical resource is under duress due to cotton crop. Cotton requires huge land mass for cultivation, ample supply of fresh water & use of pesticides for the crop. Adding to this huge impact is the issue of whether the cotton is traded under fair means? Within India in Maharashtra the Vidarbha region witnesses' suicides by farmers each year who are mainly the cotton growers. There are several cases of water issues and farmers committing suicide specifically in the cotton producing belts of India. The land mass usage for the crop cultivation, use of pesticide to protect the crop degrades the quality of soil and also the crop strips soil of its natural nutrients. According to the study undertaken by World Wild Life Foundation it takes about 2,700 liters of water to make 1 Cotton T-shirt which is what a person requires to drink for about 500 days. It further requires a lot of energy for manufacture, process, transport, wash and dry. Washing the T-shirt after use further consumes water. And this cycle goes on. Water scarcity hits more than 2 billion people. It is about time that the manufacturers and retailers re-think their choice of material for the garments to be made.

Resource and Environmental Profile Analysis: Polyester

The virgin polyester uses the Petro chemicals, thereby contributing to global warming from harmful greenhouse gases. Polyester however, is 100% recyclable. In addition to being recyclable, polyester fibres are now starting to be produced from post-consumer and post-industrial recycled materials. The consumption of non-renewable resources (petrochemicals) as we know is a critical resources and almost controls the world economy. There is also environmental impact through production of Polyester. Emissions during the production to air and water have a medium to high potential of causing environmental damage if discharged untreated including: heavy metal cobalt; manganese salts; sodium bromide and titanium dioxide. The cost of disposal for polyester are extremely slow as it is not biodegradable and add to the environmental impact of landfill sites in the very long term. Relatively large energy consumption in production, which has far-reaching environmental implications, the most serious of which includes global warming.

Considering the two studies mentioned above for Cotton and Polyester, it becomes imperative to gradually start moving towards options that will help stabilize the widespread use of Cotton and Polyester as material choice for making textile and clothing.

Opportunities that can be Explored Further to Create Better Utilization of Resources

Fabrics of all compositions can be used again. Depending on the whether it is natural or manmade the technology for recycling will vary. But the point it textiles are 100% recyclable. Regeneration fibers is a modern approach and suits the current needs of the industry. It is up to the retails and brands to give it a push by using it in contemporary techniques. The use of recycled and re-generated fibers is a big opportunity window for the textile and clothing manufacturers. Such an implementation will not just improve the sustainability of product but also will boost the image of the company. Several high street brands like H&M, Marks and Spencer, GAP and also Hyper brands like Wal-Mart are working towards bringing a change by using recycled and regenerated fabrics in their collection.

Using the Best Practices to Achieve Highest Efficiency in Fabric Cutting

The theory of Zero Wastage and Low Impact garments is a suitable solution when one is dealing with the materials that have a high impact on environment during manufacture. The wastages for mass production varies anywhere between 15% to 30%. The CAD does help in minimizing wastage but it is finally how the pattern has been created, which fabric width has been selected for optimum utilization and involvement of the technician to create the best marker for the cutting will only help to reduce the wastage. One such example is the Nike 'Low Impact Tee' which was pre-designed right from the conceptual stage to final execution where the waste percentage was just 2%. It definitely required meticulous exercise in CAD by the technician to achieve the set target.

One such task is also being undertaken by Mr. Timo Rissanen, (9) who is completing a doctorate at the University of Technology Sydney (his dissertation is titled, 'Fashion Creation Without Fabric Waste Creation'), The goal is to create jeans that are as close to zero waste as possible but that are also good looking. 'I basically had to learn to design again,' Mr. Rissanen said of his initial forays into zero waste. 'The first year and a half was a lot of trial and error.'

One way to eliminate waste is to create a garment patterns that are with details like collars, pockets, plackets, gussets and panels. These details almost fit a puzzle and help in optimization of material. Draping is another technique, like the ever elegant Indian Sari – simply by not cutting the fabric at all, but drape it directly onto the body by tucking, layer and pinning.

Anuj Sharma from Button Masala has a unique approach where is just works with some rubber bands and all sorts of buttons. Each outfit is unique and the user can keep making as many variations as he/she wants. This could be one of the approaches that can be tested on a larger audience.

Doodlage is another brand from Delhi that uses surplus fabrics from orders and creates contemporary designs for the youth. The products are not just limited to clothing but also accessories. The brand also gives a DIY and Fix it yourself kit that allows the user to repair small damages. Another option is to use fabric scraps to decorate a garment with curlicues and flowers. Excess fabric could also be used to make something entirely new (American Apparel, for example, has used excess material to create accessories and underwear). But Mr. Rissanen said the challenge of zero waste is to keep the design driven by function. In some ways, zero waste is not new. Throughout history, consumers have had to adopt similar practices, such as rationing during wars, when women fashioned new outfits from old ones. Also, classic hobbies, like knitting and quilting, can be zero-waste endeavors. Indeed, Mr. Rissanen became interested in the concept about six years ago, when he was studying 19th-and 20th-century designers like Madeleine Vionnet, a French dressmaker known for her use of the bias cut, whose work suggested that zero waste was possible. Additionally, his family has always gravitated toward what one might charitably call sustainable practices. Or as Mr. Rissanen put it: 'I'm from a very thrifty family.' 'We're offended by 15 percent waste in fabric,' Mr. Simon Collins, dean of the school of fashion at Parsons said. 'We believe in great design. But we don't believe in wasting clothes.'

Increasing the Life Cycle of the Garment

Cultures around the globe have had established and encourage a beautiful connect between a garment and its user. Heirloom clothes are the best example wherein the life cycle of the garment increases by several years if not decades. The entire concept is to have clothes that you can wear for 50 years and then followed by your child for next 50 years. It has to be made so well that it can be passed down for many years. Heirloom stitching requires use of good quality fabric, giving lining and fusing to support the fabric and keep it away from wear and tear. It is also advisable to have opening that are with buttons of tie ups for easy mending and alterations. The hem should have ample widths to keep updating the length of wearer. Heirloom clothes also add certain emotion connect with garment which in turn creates a bond with wearer.

In India, heirloom clothing has been practiced since many decades specially the beautifully woven silk and brocade saris that get passed to generations on. Creating such exquisite product requires

Reduce, Recycle and Reuse

Fashion like several other industries is centered around the user. Creating awareness and understanding in the user community and the consumer group can be one important pathway. Involving the consumer at the grass root level will create a stream that brings change. Several small ideas like working on consumption pattern, looking at fashion as not just trends but also an investment. In India, this can be lead with an example where years old Patola's and Banarasi sarees are passed on from generation to generation as an heirloom.

Cognizance of user can be further developed by workshops among user and promotion of practices that help save on essential resources of Land and Water.

The user can separate their garments in three groups:

- Clothes/accessories that can be reworn – these need not be worn directly by the 1st user. These could be a source for second hand usage.
- Reuse of existing products – Clothing and textiles that are no longer suitable to wear and could be converted into other products, such as cleaning cloths, linen etc
- Recycle – Clothing and textiles that can't be reused could be turned into textile fibres through simple processes or can be used to manufacture products such as insulating materials for the auto industry, fillers for packaging.

RESEARCH METHODOLOGY

Buying new clothes is inevitable. In this time and age advising the Mass population to cut down on the number of purchases that they make is telling someone to stop eating a Mac-Donald or any other fast food restaurant. As quoted by Albert Einstein 'We can't solve problems by using the same kind of thinking we used when we created them.'(2)

In this paper the author has started by studying the clothing that is retailed by the high street brand. The brands that were selected are – Marks and Spencer's and H&M the reason being that the fabric composition of all the garments available on the website are clearly mentioned, be it blend or solid composition.

Sample Size: the author has studied 220 garments; the research is focused specifically to understand the fabric composition for this sample size. The sample has clothing for casual and work wear for both men and women. Women's wear sampling includes – Knits: T-Shirts, Tops and Skirts, Woven: Shirts and trousers, Men's wear Knits: T-shirts, Casual Pants, Woven: Formal and Casual Shirts. The Price range for the women's band is from 9$ to 49.95$ and Men's wear price band is from 9.95$ to 55.95$.

FINDINGS AND CONCLUSION

As this research indicates, all operations during the life cycle of a product have some environmental and energy effects. Implementation of certain guide lines for textile and clothing manufacturers can improve the overall consumption pattern for the natural material.

The research indicates that there is a high consumption pattern of the material that involves high usage of environment resources. The focus should revolve on not just environmental protection but understand the production and retail patterns that lead to user consumption. A collaborative effort will bring about small and gradual changes. Holistic evaluation and realistic approaches towards environment and resources protection could be a strong direction.

'Morally, we know more sustainable clothing is the right thing to do, but we are more and more convinced that commercially it is the right thing as well,' Mike Barry, head of corporate social responsibility at Marks & Spencer, one of Britain's largest retailers. Infact it's the marketing the 'green' value of clothing, even if costs a bit more, may provide an advantage over competitors. This can be seen clearly from an example lead by H&M.

The research indicated that the Cotton and Polyester still remain to be the material of high preference for the retailers. There is a gradual shift that is showing the acceptance of materials that have lesser impact on the natural resources.

As designers and fashion consumers it imperative to understand that Fashion as a Design practice could be impact focused and not just trend led. There is a need for new ideas to arise for ways to restore environment and society, these will become the drivers for innovation and emerge from diverse locations, collaborative working relationships and cultures, rather than from being just influenced by trends. Progression towards newer materials, techniques and lifestyle will be most essential to sustain the fashion growth.

REFERENCES

[1] Defination by oxford dictionary, http://www.oxforddictionaries.com

[2] http://designerati.wordpress.com/2010/02/03/50-inspiring-quotes-on-design/

[3] Berry, W. (1990), What People are For? Berkeley, Calif: North Point Press.

[4] http://video.nationalgeographic.co.in/video/environment/freshwater/cott on-tshirts/

[5] Paper Presented Global Monthly Water Scarcity: Blue Water Footprints versus Blue Water Availability, Arjen Y. Hoekstra, Mesfin M. Mekonnen, Ashok K. Chapagain, Ruth E. Mathews, Brian D. Richter.

[6] Resource and Environmental Profile Analysis of a Manufactured Apparel Product Life Cycle Analysis (LCA): Woman's Knit Polyester Blouse (June 1993). Prepared for American Fiber Manufacturers Association by Franklin Associates Ltd.

[7] http://www.uniformreuse.co.uk/

[8] Cradle to Cradle® is a registered trademark of McDonough Braungart Design Chemistry.

[9] http://www.nytimes.com/2010/08/15/fashion/15waste.html?pagewanted=all and http://zerofabricwastefashion.blogspot.in/

[10] http://corporate.marksandspencer.com/

[11] Anon (2018), [online] available at: http://about.hm.com/en/About/Sustainability/Commitments/Reduce-Reuse-Recycle/Garment-Collecting.html [Accessed 5 Feb. 2018].

[12] Anon (2018), [online] available at: http://Reuse-Recycle/Garment-Collecting.html [Accessed 5 Feb. 2018].

[13] Fletcher, K. & Grose, L. (2012). Fashion & Sustainability – Design for Change. Laurence King Publishing Ltd.

ANNEXURE

Brand – Marks and Spencer

Category – Women's Knitwear

Research finding – Cotton and Polyester seen as the choice of material for the clothing under this category

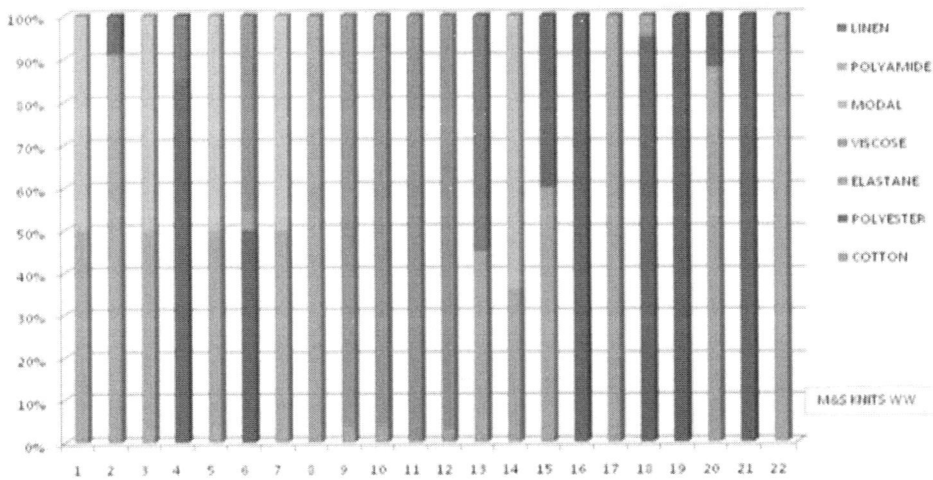

Brand – Marks and Spencer

Category – Women's Woven clothing

Research finding – Cotton and Polyester seen as the choice of material for the clothing under this category

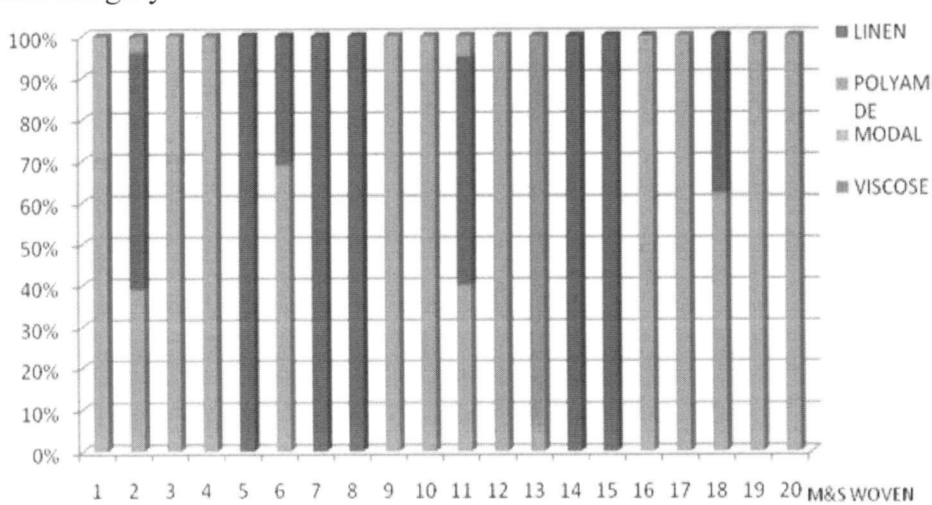

Brand – Marks and Spencer
Category – Men's Woven clothing
Research finding – Cotton and Polyester seen as the choice of material for the clothing under this category

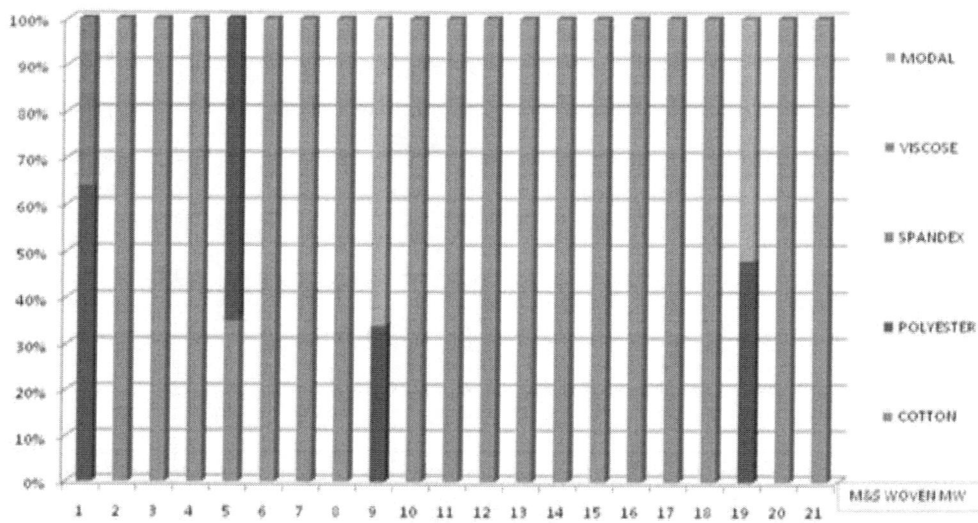

Brand – H&M
Category – Women's Knitwear
Research finding – Cotton and Polyester seen as the choice of material for the clothing under this category

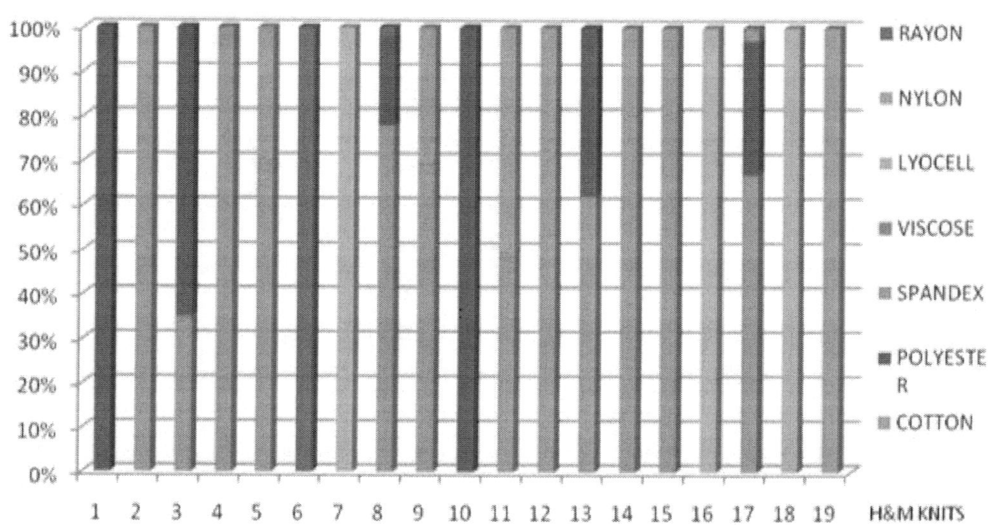

Brand – H&M
Category – Women's Skirts
Research finding – Polyester seen as the choice of material for the clothing under this category

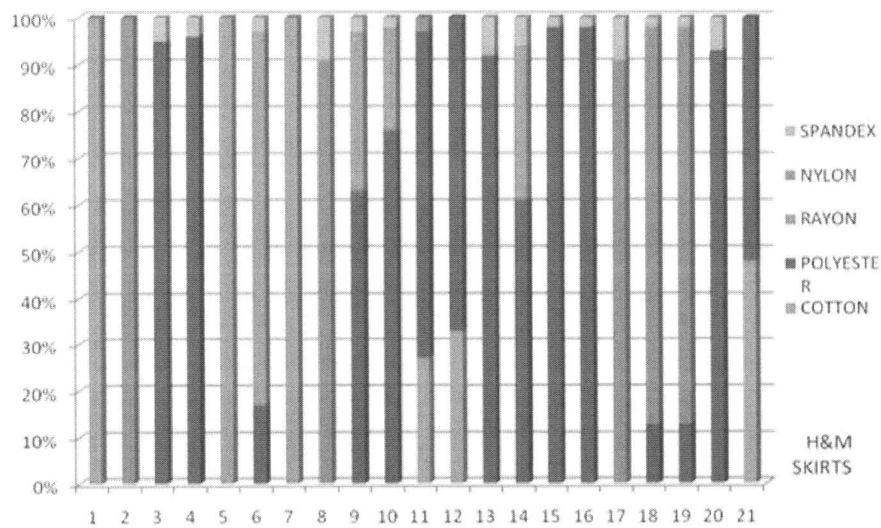

Brand – H&M
Category – Women's Tops
Research finding – Rayon seen as the choice of material for the clothing under this category

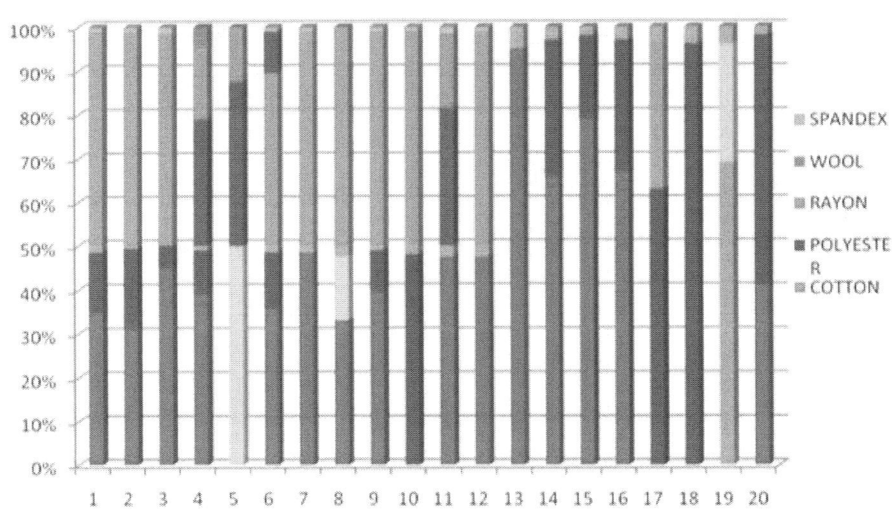

Brand – H&M
Category – Men's Woven clothing
Research finding – Cotton and Polyester seen as the choice of material for the clothing under this category

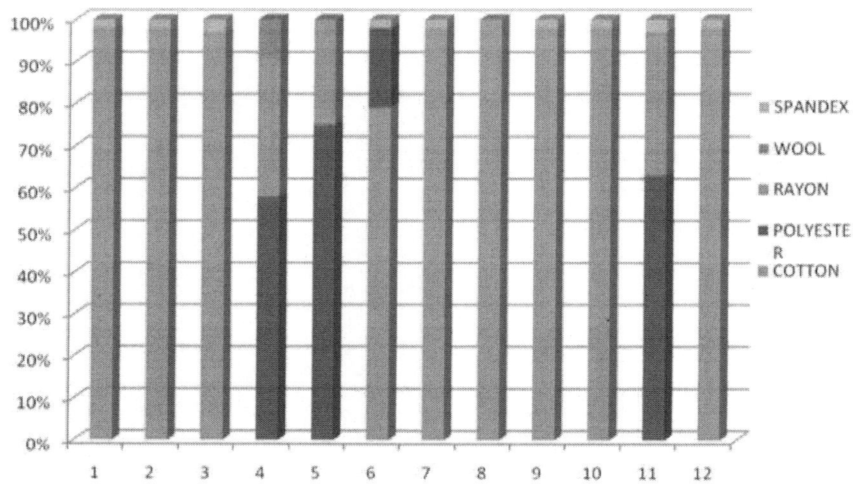

Brand – H&M
Category – Men's Woven clothing
Research finding – Cotton seen as the choice of material for the clothing under this category

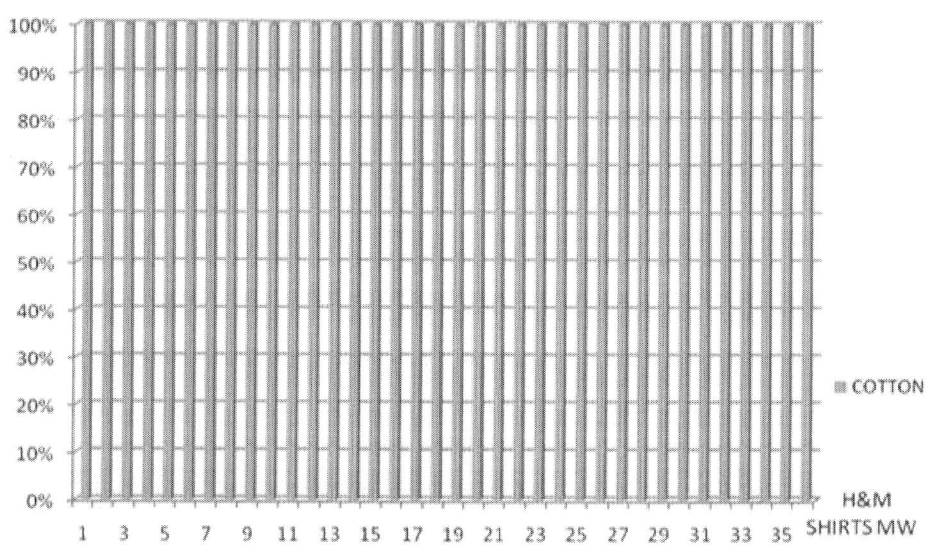

Consolidated report on usage of different material again shows Cotton leading in usage

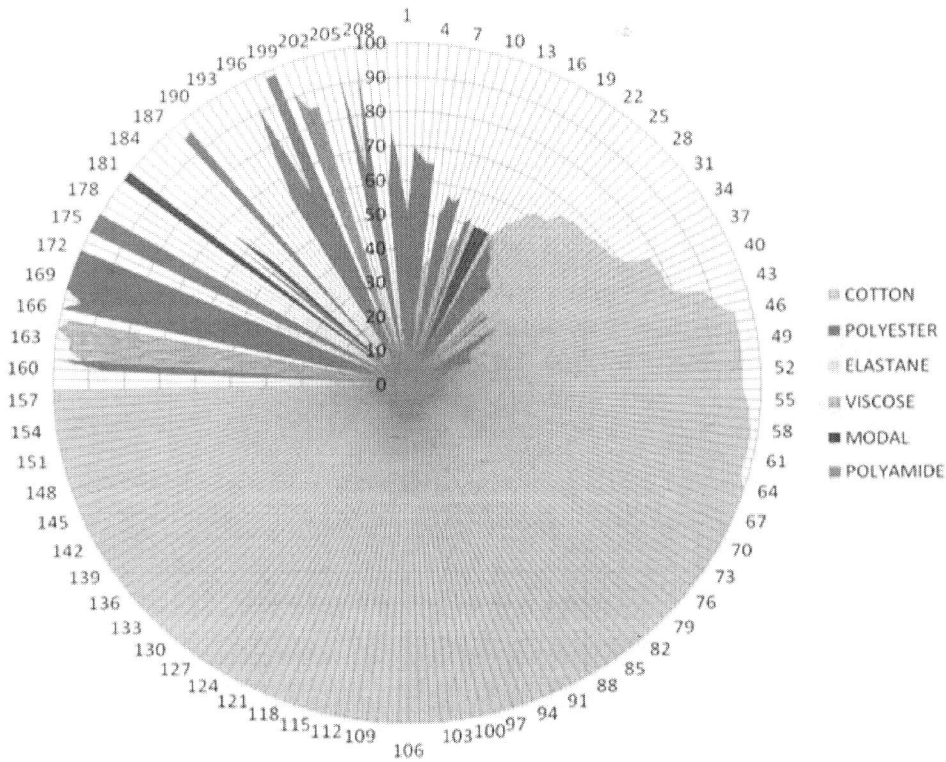

Refusing Waste – Anticipation of Social and Political Behaviours (MODUS)

Reframing Resources between the Circle of Creation, Preservation and Disruption

BARBARA ALEJANDRA PINO AHUMADA

Faculty of Architecture, Art, Design, FAAD, Diego Portales University, Santiago, Chile

E-mail: barbara.pino@udp.cl

ABSTRACT

Today the words 'sustainability and waste' are worldwide spread: it is a buzz often used according a millenaristic meaning, announcing the end of the world for the ozone hole growth, the clime changes, the 'big patch', and so on.

Researchers, ecologist and media cry against the pollution and the residuals, invoking new kinds of production. The same reads the financial newspapers in order to verify how to invest their money, possibly respecting sustainability. The problem is deeper: we need to survive to the cultural and social changes imposed by our systemic approaches, also if sustainable.

This paper wants to stimulate a philosophical debate an this topics, pointing out how much the best innovations, technological or not, provided disruption 'change' of stable behaviours, determining uncontrolled residual wasting, mainly social and cultural.

Keywords: *Critical thinking, Disruptive design, Design for anticipation, Autopoietic society, Design leadership.*

INTRODUCTION

In our present western culture, we consider residuals as a problem, and the current thought points out the need to avoid as much as possible the generation of waste, but nature and evolution think quit different: residuals are life. But nature works on long times, and adaptation of the environment in order to find new equilibria is possible, humans make changes in present times not compliant with the evolution time, and waste can determine locally, and possibly permanently, mutations of the environment.

Moreover, we are so arrogant that think possible to change global natural equilibria through human activities, and provide alarms about global pollution, global warming, change of the climate due to anthropic activities, and so on.

In front of the continuous flow of economic challenges, the industrial design system has to adapt, criticise and evolve in close connection with the incoming changes. If previously design was seen as a professional activity and a discipline combining aesthetics and pragmatism (Simon), throughout time this activity generated its own ecology that abides to the rules of self-referential, living entities.

In order to demystify the idea of a smoothly working, virtuous and sustainable design, it is necessary to reconsider the 'un-clean' and imperfect nature of exchanges in the biological, social and economic environment and face the environmental mutations and overall damage created by this stereotype. The paper will unfold in three main concepts:

1. the debris, anomaly and residuals will be shown as manifestations of the natural exchanges and therefore integral part of the living environment, allowing the long term anticipation of its evolution, or futuring 'CREATION'.
2. it will be shown how by emarginating and ignoring the importance of debris, the sustainable design discourse deviated from the logic of the living mechanisms. In this context will be argue that design became a self-referential system defuturing 'PRESERVATION' in this way the outcomes of its activity.
3. will be propose that looking at design as an activity that radically changed and will continue to provoke mutations to the environment will help re-futuring 'DISRUPTION' sustainable design theory.

FROM ANTICIPATION TO THE ILLUSION OF SUSTAINABILITY AND THE ENVIRONMENTAL MUTATIONS.

The future of productive innovations is a long debated theme that changed throughout the years. Starting from the advances of mass production technologies and the fordist approach based on industrialisation and standardisation (Smith, 1994) to the luddist approach (Randall, 1997) in which the fear of technology innovation generates fringe behaviours, design and sustainability developed in parallel with the changes in the environment. (ACTIVISM)

This evolution was so far seen as a reaction to the actual state of the art of the ecological mutations, and passed from the imaginary of living with the hope and ignoring the impact of the industrial and economic fast pace advances, futuring a world that slowly adapts to the inputs of the human activity, to the illusion that the living environment takes care of its own balance no matter the damage created by the economic growth, and though defuturing the human activity, to the acknowledgement of the mutations as an integral part of the environment's lifecycle.

Re-futuring is therefore seen as the act of dismantling the stereotype of sustainability as a circle of virtuous behaviours, extending it to the integrate the debris and refusal as intrinsic parts of the living environment (Fig.1).

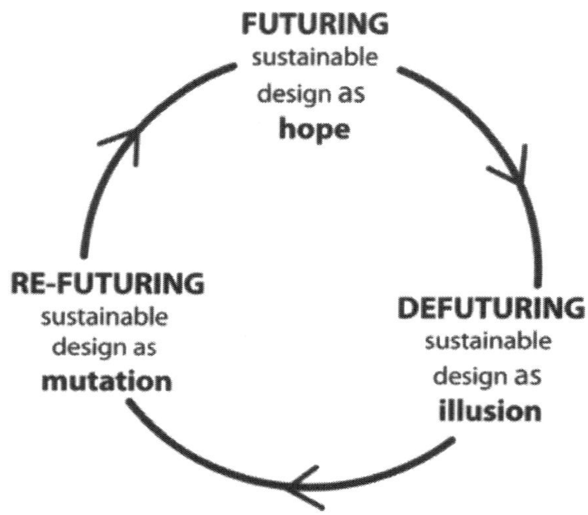

Figure 1: Futuring, Defuturing and Re-futuring

In fact, we can consider any kind of human (and not only) activity as shown in the following scheme:

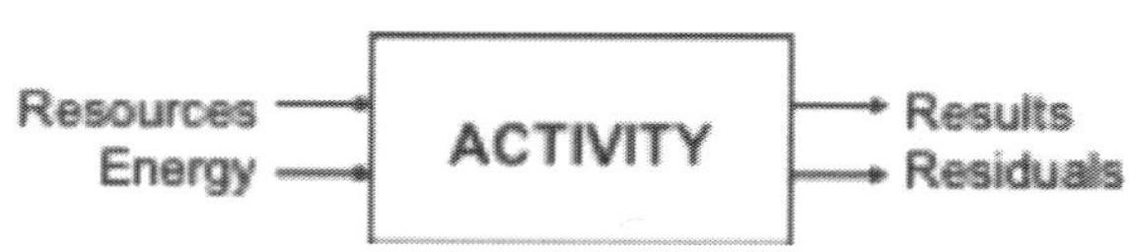

Figure 2: Human Activity Flow

In our present western culture, we consider residuals as a problem, and the current thought points out the need to avoid as much as possible the generation of waste, but nature and evolution think quit different: residuals are life.

But nature works on long times, and adaptation of the environment in order to find new equilibria is possible, humans make changes in times not compliant with the evolution time, and waste can determine locally, and possibly permanently, disruptive changes. More, we are so arrogant that think possible to change global natural equilibria through human activities, and provide alarms about global pollution, global warming, change of the climate due to anthropic activities, and so on. While crying so huge problems, and caring to design sustainable products and services, we do not observe other normal, common actions, producing different kinds of waste, affecting dramatically both our life and society.

Figure 3 presents the typical industrial production:

Figure 3: The Scheme of a Typical Industrial Activity

It implies the use of a capital, in order to transform commodities into added value products through manpower, and among the outputs we will find, beside the economic gain, also residuals: those residuals are often source of pollution, and are the main care of sustainability prophets.

Figure 4: The Typical Effect of the Technology Growth

Also ideas and cultural contents are affected by processes changing them, and then producing residuals (Fig. 5).

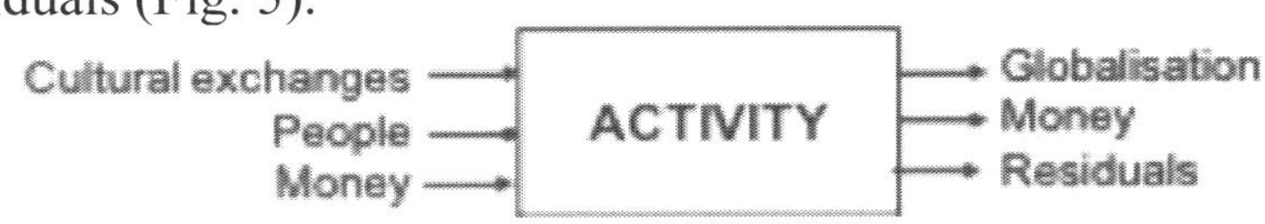

Figure 5: Globalisation

For example, the large diffusion of internet, of internet services imposed many changes in the way of thinking economy, finance, work and so on. Today, we consider the national economy and the production of working places in a quite different way as our parents was doing. The actual model could be roughly represented as in Fig. 6.

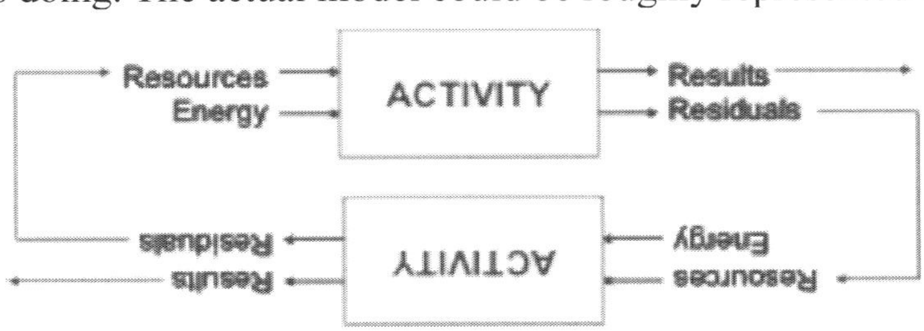

Figure 6: Two Different Processes Interacting and then Building a Situation in which the Free Residuals and the Free Resources are Properly Balanced

CAN WE MANAGE SOCIAL RESIDUALS AS USUAL GARBAGE?

Is it possible to approach the problem of social, cultural environmental residuals as we do for the products? Of course, we can do. As Design enlarged its action areas from products to communication, services, and in general to many artefacts coping with social changes, we can observe the typical approaches for reducing the traditional residuals and approaching them as design problems.

- **Reduce.** Reduce the quantity of residuals produced.
- **Repair.** If something is damaged, repair it, instead of replacing it with a new one.
- **Reuse.** If something is obsolete, find a way to make it useful, also in a different context.
- **Recycle.** If something is to be throw out, recover as much as possible of the materials inside.

Unfortunately, faster we do, faster competitors and environment react, leaving us at the same point. It seems a phenomenon similar to a viral flu: every year the research runs at the maximum speed for producing the proper vaccine, and in the while viruses change, leaving us at the same initial point.

The fact is recalled in Through the Looking-Glass by Lewis Carroll: the Red Queen and Alice, despite are constantly running, remain always in the same place.

'*Well, in our country,*' said Alice, still panting a little, '*you'd generally get to somewhere else — if you run very fast for a long time, as we've been doing.*'

'*A slow sort of country!*' said the Queen. '*Now, here, you see, it takes all the running you can do, to keep in the same place. If you want to get somewhere else, you must run at least twice as fast as that!*' (Carroll, L. 1972, p. 36).

Which is the residual in this process? Possibly our time: we are wasting time in producing information we don't have for who don't care, in searching for the appearance of results instead of for solid and durable results, in accumulating money to have expenditure capability instead of creating solid richness able to influence a community, and so on.

But time flows, and we cannot apply the 4 R's rules to it. In order to avoid this unrecoverable residual, we have to return back, and think to the residual "proper speed", discarded by the technologies. Proper speed does not mean to be slow, but to accept that there are different valuable durations for different situations: while to be healed from a illness quickly is valuable, it is not so in feeling pleasures. In the following we refer to 'slowness' to intend the opposite of the complex mix of success-speed-appearance.

Here some examples.

Reduce. Being the technologies and the mechanism audience-success-money of the media the factors wasting the idea of 'proper time', in order to reduce such residual, we should reduce the use of unnecessary technologies, and support the pleasure of participation (J. Panksepp, L. Biven, 2012). This is matter of cultural education and public services, for making easier the contacts in presence and collaborative activities.

Repair. You cannot break an idea, but you can make it unusable in a context. To repair an idea means to remodel it according to new constraints. In the case of 'slowness', it is in fact often worthless: taking one hour travelling on a bus for reaching a place in a crowded town is boring, stressing and worthless, but using the same time for the same purpose providing valuable experiences could be desirable. It is matter to complement the primary service with emotioning activities. In this example, the 'slowness' is repaired locally, but this approach could be a systematic principles, to apply in a generalised way. Being in any case 'slowness' an idea, a point of view, education is still a relevant element for repairing it.

Reuse. 'Slowness' is associated to more thought decisions, to reduction of impulsivity, then, often, to reduction of errors. We could so apply more 'slowness' to any production process. If global constraints impose to us speed and quick success, we can 'immerge' the corporate processes, forced to look to the next quarter, into new observation (and then ruling) processes looking and measuring the behaviours as a low-pass filter, cutting spikes, and then better understanding trends. We can reuse slowness abstracting it and making of it a metamodel. Again, what is behind is a change of the values implying education.

Recycle. To recycle means to extract parts of the residuals in order to reuse them in new productions. So, to recycle 'slowness' we have to decompose it into parts, and reuse the single ideas/principles. In what we called 'slowness' we can find the ability to taste pleasure, taking the required time; pleasure can be obtained in different ways, but there are primary actions giving us it: investigation, study, play, love, social co-operation, etc. (J. Panksepp, L. Biven, 2012).

COACHING ADAPTIVE DESIGN THINKING (MODUS) TO CRITICISE AND INTERPRET IMPOSED SCENARIO

'Fighting with a large army under your command is nowise different from fighting with a small one: it is merely a question of instituting signs and signals.'

– Sun Tzu, *The art of war and strategy* (Tzu, S. 2007)

Contrasting the design thinking approach that, the design attitude operates as a deconstructive strategy in itself and not as a tool employed to reinforce the adaptive skills. By using the lateral thinking 'MODUS' specific to the design training and seeking the meaning of the conflictual situations, the design principles have the potential to develop the necessary codes that enable control and leadership of the creative process.

More specifically thinking of design as a pro-active attitude 'MODUS', empowers the new generation of designers to take leadership and use design not as an accessory to support the established norms but as a strategy of criticise that can open the opportunity for change.

To fully understand the potential and limits of a Adaptive Design Thinking 'MODUS' it is useful divide the possible actions into two different modalities (Fig. 7). This means an alteration of the present norms and rules in order to influence and manage the territory of intervention through persuasion, requires indirect actions that are not necessary explicit. This kind of process calls for the continuous adjustment to the changing conditions learning how to maintain the advantage no matter the circumstances. An aggravation of the conflict brings to the complete destruction of a reasoning system. In order to achieve destruction and therefore a radical fracture with the old norms, an attitude of leadership has to prevail through the imposition of power. Contrasting the management of the internal dynamics of the group, the leadership behaviour and attitude aims at a more rapid change.

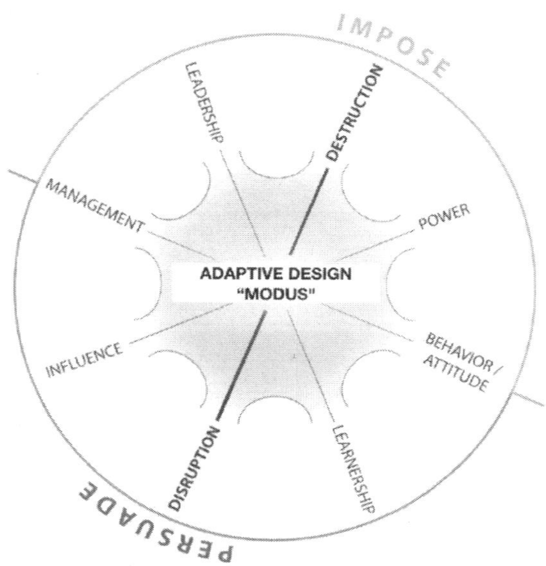

Figure 7: Adaptive Design Thinking 'MODUS' Tensions

In Design for the real world, Papanek uses the concept of Telesis to explain how products have to reflect the true conditions of the environment, translating them into meaningful design concepts. He gives as an example the crude appropriation of the Japanese artefacts without caring for the behaviour and affective value embedded in them, merely following a fashion trend (Papaneck, V. 1971).

The progress of the Adaptive Thinking is shaped by the tensions between several factors such as the exercise of power and influence, the behaviour and management that are related to a negotiation of professional design principles and way of reasoning. For this reason the actual context in which this negotiation occur is more related to the specific historical moment of global crisis rather than an actual precise working environment such a firm or an agency. The physical context in this sense influences and provides stimulus but is not determinant in the disruption process.

The negotiation process can be seen from two different perspectives: first as a collaborative process with a fairly stable characteristic, in which consensus prevails, and that encounters occasional breakdowns, and second as a state of unsettlement in which consensus is seen as a temporary agreement. The breakdown is intended as outlined by Flores et al. as

> *that participants might assess as negative (as when the pen you are writing with runs out of ink) or as a positive new opportunity (e.g., a stray useful thought that interrupts your flow of writing or a friend knocking at the door).* (Flores, F. 1988, p. 156)

While the first perspective is usually preferred in the design collaboration literature, it also presents an idealistic facet of the reality. The second perspective however, comes closer to the actual struggle encountered in real-life situations in which the circumstances are in a continuous flow. It is at this point that the Adaptive Thinking 'MODUS' has to be understood as a liberating factor, unleashing tensions and making place for creativity.

CONCLUSION

Started from considering and re-proposing the paradigm of futuring introduced by Tony Fry in 2009 in the realm of the design activity as a lens to read and reveal the change in the imaginary of sustainability and its passage from hope to illusion and to mutation, moreover introduced the term re-futuring as a way to envision the continuous a mutation in the future and the impossibility to predict the consequences of the ongoing design innovation and the anomaly they will generate in a longer time span. As a way to understand the dynamics behind the creation of debris and anomaly has been proposed that design has to be looked at as a self-referential creative system whose interactive exchanges happen in a chaotic manner and react to internal factors and external alterations.

The introduction of the design as a creative self-referential system triggers the acknowledgement of the paradoxical relation between virtuous and vicious, creation preservation and destruction as being intimately connected and consistent parts of any living system. In this sense the manifestations of the living systems cannot be attached a positive of negative value because they intrinsically contain both good and evil.

The only way to get this Adaptive Thinking is a strong leadership, able to Criticise, Interpret and Define clear strategies, to manage in the best ways the resources and commodities and and the remaining debris, reinterpreting and integrating them into a parallel process of social, cultural and political change.

Starting from the integration of design thinking and design practice into the design leadership mind frame as a possible approach for coaching design leaders with Adaptive Thinking "MODUS".

Drawing from design management literature, has been argued that due to the emergence of new business realities designers are required in leadership roles. This position asks for a mutated awareness, which shifts from the individual focus to the overall acknowledgement of the organisational system and environment. This holistic approach calls for expert designers to learn about their own strengths and weaknesses, and learn to cultivate critical capabilities. I conclude by suggesting that although design leadership is still a relatively new concept in the design discipline literature, coaching Adaptive Thinking 'MODUS' can be successfully implemented and maybe we have the duty to rethink the problem of cultural and human residuals: Refusing Waste, Reframing with Critical thinking 'MODUS'.

REFERENCES

[1] Papanek, V. (1971), *Design for the Real World: Human Ecology and Social Change*, New York, Pantheon Books.

[2] Carroll, L. (1972), *Through the Looking-Glass and What Alice Found There*. Macmillan.

[3] Tzu, S. (2007), *The Art of War and Strategy*. Milano, Rizzoli.

[4] Flores, F., Graves, M., Hartfield, B., & Winograd, T. (1988), Computer Systems and the

Design of Organizational Interaction. *ACM Transactions on Information Systems (TOIS)*, 6(2), 153-172.

[5] Cross, N. (2004), Expertise in Design: An Overview. *Design Studies*, 25(5), 427-441.

[6] Borja De Mozota, B. (2003), *Design Management*, New York.

[7] Fry, T. (2010), *Design as Politics*. Berg.

[8] Langton, C.G. (ed.) (1997), *Artificial Life: An Overview*. MIT Press.

[9] Latour, B. (1987), Science in Action: How to Follow Scientists and Engineers through Society. Harvard University Press.

[10] Manzini, E. (2007), Design Research for Sustainable Social Innovation. *Design Research Now*, 233-245.

[11] Simon, H.A. (1969), *The Sciences of the Artificial* (Vol. 136). MIT press.

[12] Smith, T. (1994), Making the Modern: Industry, Art, and Design in America. University of Chicago Press.

[13] Wenger, E. (1998), Communities of Practice: Learning, Meaning, and Identity. Cambridge University Press.

[14] Panksepp, J. & Biven, L. (2012), The Archaeology of Mind: Neuroevolutionary Origins of Human Emotions (Norton Series on Interpersonal Neurobiology). New York: WW Norton & Company.

[15] Randall, A. (1997), Reinterpreting 'Luddism': Resistance to New Technology in the British. *Resistance to New Technology: Nuclear Power, Information Technology and Biotechnology*, 57.

Industry Initiatives for Waste Transformation

BEATRICE FRIGO AND EUGENIA CHIARA
Politecnico di Milano, Italy
E-mail: beatrice.frigo@mail.polimi.it; eugenia.chiara@polimi.it

ABSTRACT

Recently, the fashion industry has shown a significative growth of interest toward sustainability and transparency in terms of production, environment, communication.

Whether this is just a commercial move to follow the trend, or a serious loyalty to social and environmental issues, we have to admit the big steps the fashion world made in the last 5 years, and how much this issue is influencing the productive trend.

Any loop of the productive and supply chain of the industry investigated on their responsibilities and took different initiative, such as deeper care on the dying process, a wider promotion of organic cotton, a stricter control of the labor condition, just to list some.

But what about the ending phase of the fashion product and its dismission?

We were all shocked by the last fw17 Stella Mc Cartney campaign set in a landfill, we all felt less guilty when we brought our unused clothes to a "take back" spot in the H&M store, and we all wished to can wear the new Adidas Parley to save the oceans from plastic bottles.

Those are just some of the initiatives for fashion waste sensibiliization but they are like an iceberg point of a more and more structured fashion waste transformation industry.

In this perspective, man-made fibers can play a more interesting role for a never-ending transformation of the matter, as some advanced textile company can prove, but also the possibility of biodegradable fabrics opens the scene to new conceptions of the waste.

Waste can be a great resource for the industry and for the whole planet, cause, quoting the design theory Cradle to Cradle, the waste is food, just as in nature.

All those initiatives are designed also to bring advantages to the brand itself, both in the brand image and in the product quality, and they weight a lot in the costumer's perception of the company.

Keywords: *Fashion, Waste, Transformation.*

INTRODUCTION

The fashion industry has recently shown a significant growth of interest toward sustainability and transparency in terms of production, environment, and trade.

Whether this is just a commercial move to follow the trend, or a serious loyalty to the cause, we must admit the big steps the fashion world made in the last decade, thanks to the improvements of the industrial technologies and the consumer's awareness.

Essential has been the Greenpeace Detox Commitment of 2011 signed by many fashion brands that oblige them to show publicly their updated commitments and certified initiatives toward sustainability.

There are many ways a fashion product can be sustainable: the choice of the raw material, the transformation and the finishing, the labor condition, the logistic, the maintenance, and least but not last, the dismission.

This paper wants to examine the current situation of brands' initiatives for fashion waste and its transformation as an advantage for the industry itself.

CONTEXT ANALYSIS

The latest report about the environmental impacts of the clothing industry led in the UK (Valuing Our Clothes: the cost of UK fashion, Wrap, July 2017) reveals that clothing has the 4th environmental impact after housing, transportation and food.

Comparing the previous report published in 2012, the current research underlines that the volume of clothes bought rose by nearly 200,000 tons to 1.13 million tons in 2016.

Although the amount of clothing being sent to landfill has fallen by 14% from 350,000 tons in 2012 to 300,000 in 2016: a one-quarter is still binned rather than recycled (31% just as four years ago).

But the data are terribly worse if we consider BRIC countries (Brazil, Russia, India, China) where the dimensions and the prospective to grow are much bigger.

For instance, only 4 years ago in China 26 million tons of textile waste originating from industry and consumers was generated every year (according to China Association of Resource Comprehensive Utilization) and an average of 217 tons of textiles were estimated to enter Hong Kong's landfills every day in 2011 (according to Hong Kong's Environmental Protection Department).

In front of this scenario, waste transformation is no more an optional for the industry and consumers. This is the reason why many brands, agencies, companies took on this new challenge. But before going on discovering the initiatives born into fashion system, it's necessary to take a step back and clarify what we mean by fashion waste.

There are 2 big families of waste in fashion: the pre-consumption and the post-consumption waste.

The former includes all the production scraps generated during the cutting and sewing process, together with the cones of thread, the mockups, and the samples.

The latter counts the unwanted, unused or unusable garments after being used but also the defected items and the unsold ones.

The post-industrial waste of the pre-consumption category can be recycled or reduced to its minimum, following the zero-waste fashion movement and through a relevant role of the design.

For instance, by designing perfectly the patterns and by taking care of other design details is possible to avoid scraps in the production, just as brands as Elementum by Daniela Pais and Make/Use demonstrated.

Otherwise, the production scraps can get another chance to be used through brands like Progetto Quid and Mark Liu, whereas the samples or defected items can reach a new opportunity thanks to platforms like Sempleness and company like PreLoved.

Without this design intervention, the scraps would be reused for other purpose, recycled by some special textile company, or brought to landfill.

About the recycling of the post-consumption waste, there are many companies born to manage it, apart from the charity and humanitarian channels.

CO is a Switzerland-based company that is specialized in shoe and clothing recycling. It organizes the recollection of discarded fashion items through the bins of the 'take back' campaigns but also directly from fashion factories. H&M is its biggest partner, but also brands like The North Face, Levi's, and Forever 21, Intimissimi, C&A collaborate with I: CO constantly.

The company manages the transport, the storage and the transformation into new material towards a closed loop manufacturing cycle, aiming to redesign the life cycle of the fashion product.

WASTE TRANSFORMATION

In front of the waste problematic, the fashion system gave different answers, under the pression of the public opinion. We must keep in mind that the first step for any change in fashion is made by the material innovation, and surely the development of new technologies in the fiber recycling helped enormously in the development of new system of waste transformation.

So it's thanks to textile companies like ECONYL®, Cardato Recycled®, RecoveTex®, RadiciGroup and many others if today we can have some worthy cases of study.

Their efforts in updating their productive process and their constant research on their R&D department have been essential to permit a wider scenario of sustainable solutions in terms of material, finishing, dying and recycling.

The ECONYL® Regeneration System is an industrial system created by Aquafil Group in 2011, that turns waste into first-grade Nylon 6.

The raw material used in this production system comes from post-consumer waste (end- of-life products made from Polyamide 6 such as fishing nets, carpet fluff, hosiery and rigid textiles) but also pre-consumer waste (oligomers, scraps and other plastic components generated from the production of Nylon 6).

The yarn that comes out from this process is made from 100% regenerated materials and 100%. The regenerated Nylon 6 yarn is used in final products such as garments and synthetic carpet flooring.

A project of this magnitude required the investment of more than 20 million euro, a new plant in Slovenia, the development of new technologies, supply chains, efficient networks and logistic and successful partnerships.

The company admits that it hasn't been easy, but in few years ECONYL® gains a lot of prestigious clients like Levi's, Adidas, Triumph, Volcom.

Stylish clothes, accessories, hosiery and lingerie are all types of garments that can be created from ECONYL® fibers, but also high-performance sportswear, swimwear, and outdoor apparel.

New fashion green start-up are enthusiastically using this material for their production.

The hosiery brand Swedish Stocking creates stocking using ECONYL® regenerated nylon. Their mission is to change and influence the entire hosiery industry, since now pantyhose is a petroleum product and one of our biggest consumables.

The production process they are using is a lot less harmful to the environment than traditional nylon production and with their 'take back' campaign of old and broken pantyhose they contribute a lot in the recycling of nylon, therefore in the production of material of new stockings.

But good news is not only for man-made fibers.

3C Filati is one of the Italian companies of the Prato District that produces recycled wool under the strict certification of Cardato Recycled.

This specific technique of producing yarn from old clothing knit is called recycled carding and consists in the blending of short rescued fibers of different lengths and composition.

Once the pure virgin wool was absolutely the most precious requirement for wool garment, but nowadays the sensibility to green issues is moving the trend towards regenerated processes that permits the rescue of the original beauty of the wool.

A luxury brand like Trenery promotes regenerated Cashemere named Filpucci's ninety-five, which is created from post-consumer pure fibres, plus a very small amount of extra fine merino wool, to assist with performance and colour.

In this overview of waste transformation technologies and tools, that allowed fashion brands to embrace sustainable initiatives, we can also mention the ones concerning water, CO2 and Energy recycling.

In fact, the production of a cotton T-shirt requires 2,700 liters of water, which is the quantity a person could drink for 900 days. It also takes a lot of energy to grow the cotton, to manufacture, to transport.

The Italian company Europrogetti is one of the most advanced in the design of technologies and solutions for factories' water depuration and recovery.

In 2014 they launched the Wasatex project in the Olimpias Tekstil factory (Benetton Group) in Croatia. This establishment used to produce up to 8.000 kg/day of yarn, consuming 1.600 m3/day of well water.

Thanks to the installation of the ZDL (Zero Liquid Discharge) by Europrogetti and the support of the Eco-Innovation EU project, the factory now consumes less than 1.000 m3/day.

Moreover, if we take in account that the recycled water has an average temperature of 30°C, against a temperature of 15°C of the well water, there is an energy saving in the heating up the water to the operating temperatures.

The certification of the recycling degree of the material is nowadays guaranteed by an independent agency called RE-MO (recycling movement).

RE-MO is a Dutch company initiated by textile experts, whose mission is to make recycling visible and simple, inspiring people towards sustainable consumption and conscious fashion.

With the Remo Key tool, a fun little card with a track & trace system that can be accessed through a QR code, the consumer will easily access to a website containing information about an item's origin and past life such as where and how the item is recycled, the precise percentage of recycled material and the resulting environmental savings on Water, CO2 and Energy.

This innovative platform permits a certification of guarantee and it has already been embraced by fashion brand and textile company such as Mud-Jeans, Asos Denim, Fil 3, Recovertex, Marchi&Fildi.

Now that we have a background awareness of some of the existing technologies for waste transformation we are about to pick up 3 case study of fashion brands that adopted those initiatives successfully.

The range of choice is quite wide nowadays, and it's necessary to understand the authenticity of their initiatives.

We decided to group 3 bigger families and analyze the most significant case of each one.

We selected the brands that are putting themselves more in the first line of sustainable fashion. They are all based in Europe, but they have different dimension, target and core products.

The first group takes in consideration multinational fashion brands, female oriented, pret-a -porter, in which the style has more relevance. The case study will be represented by H&M.

The second case study is about Adidas, as proponent of the wide family of sportswear fashion brands, in which innovation and functionality compete with style.

The third example wants to bring under lights the green fashion realities that have strong sustainable aims already in their DNA, that invest a lot in good design and research, and that develop new models of consumption applicable in every context, and in this case, we will show the example of Freitag. The scheme we are applying for every case study is composed by 4 points: the motivation why the brand is moving toward sustainability, the concrete initiatives it is adopting, the approach toward waste transformation, and the critics about it.

CASE STUDY 1

The collapse of Rana Plaza building in Bangladesh, on the 24th of April 2013, will be forever a marking point in the fast fashion industry. 1,138 people died, another

2,500 were injured, and all those people were involved in the production for western's fashion brands.

Tragically the medias' spotlights turned on the human and environmental effects that this massive production of cheap and fancy clothes were provoking and what brands were allowing with their indifference.

The world-wide public opinion got shocked, many were the famous brands involved, and many were the protests. Activist movements like Fashion Revolution born with the purpose to impose transparency to fashion brands and to keep the attention always high on those topics.

The Swedish multinational fashion brand H&M was one of the most involved in the inquiry, but just after that catastrophe its sensitivity about human and environmental issues changed, becoming the brand who talks about sustainability more than any other fast-fashion brand.

On its website there is a big well-explained section about sustainability, where it gives information about the material, the working condition, the wages, the building safety, the animal welfare, the chemicals and the water consumption. It also publishes the sustainable report of every year and an ambitious sustainable plan of goals to reach by 2040.

H&M started the production of a Conscious collection made by using sustainable and recycled materials, and launched the initiative 'Closing the loop' through glossy ad campaigns in order to encourage garment recycling.

Closing the loop is undeniably the first worldwide action for the waste recycling publicly ever taken, thanks to the big dimension of H&M, its capillarity and success, together with its powerful communication and promotion channels.

Karl-Johan Persson, CEO of H&M, says about the initiative, 'Creating a closed loop for textiles, in which unwanted clothes can be recycled into new ones, will not only minimize textile waste, but also significantly reduce the need for virgin resources as well as other impacts fashion has on our planet.'

Since 2013, the company says it has collected more than 25,000 tons of textile waste, and it launched an international contest looking for innovative ideas to recycle it all.

In partnership with a recycling technology company called Worn Again and the recollection system I:CO, H&M provides different treatments of the 'taken-back' clothing, sorting it into 5 different areas of further use to reach the most environmental and economical recycling result.

Re-wear: the clothing in proper condition is marketed worldwide as second-hand goods. Re-use: the no-longer suitable textiles are converted into other products such as cleaning cloths. Up cycling: the components are split and the materials that conserve resource are reused to produce new products, closing the loop.

Down cycling: when a material is no longer usable is then processed into new products such as thermal insulation. Energy: if none of the previous categories is suiting for textile waste, it is then used to produce energy.

The most successful result of waste transformation for H&M is the Recycled denim collection, launched in 2014.

Although the intents are good, still many are the contradictions run throughout H&M's business. The critics argue that H&M fights textile waste while producing massive volumes of cheap, easily disposable clothing, that it wants to reduce its environmental footprint while doubling its store footprint.

Greenpeace complains to the brand that the recycling campaign is an illusion, because only a low percentage of the collected clothing can be used as recycled fibers. 'Offering garment repair services would have done more good than inviting customers to recycle their old clothes and buy new ones' wrote in a press release Kirsten Brodde, the project lead of Greenpeace Detox My Fashion.

H&M is working hard in position itself as an industry leader in sustainability, much more than other fast-fashion brands such as Primark that does basically nothing. But in this way, it is exposing itself to skeptical critics and continuous monitoring. Surely the problem is still the business model of consume, but incremental change and pressure from the consumers do worth a lot.

CASE STUDY 2

The sportswear fashion companies are the one who are the most involved in the using of fossil-oil raw material sources, due to the high performative requirements of their fabrics that only man-made fibers can reach through engineering. But for the same reason they can also be the key for a sustainable production and a solution for the recycling industry.

'We are working with PARLEY to keep plastic out of our oceans and transform it into high-performance sportswear. Spinning the problem into a solution. The threat into thread.' This is the statement Adidas proudly announces in its website to launch the training shoe Adidas x Parley.

Parley for the Oceans is an international platform born to preserve the oceans from plastic pollution, and to support arts, science, research, industry that is taking care of this problem.

The German-based and worldwide-known brand Adidas has always been interested in sustainable issues.

In its annual public report on sustainability, the company declares to have improved transparency within its supply chain, introduced more sustainable manufacturing processes, such as its waterless Dry Dye t-shirt line, and improved energy efficiency in many of its stores. Moreover, the successful collaboration with the fashion designer Stella McCartney since 2005 has given always more a drive to improve the sustainability in the design and in the production.

Surely the most strong action Adidas lately took is the launch of a concept sneaker made from 3D-printed recycled ocean waste. The name is UltraBOOST Uncaged Parley: a reference to both the design's environmental cause and the popular UltraBOOST range of light-weight running shoes.

Each shoe's upper is made from 5 percent recycled polyester and 95 percent waste plastic dredged from the ocean around the Maldives. Each pair of shoes contains up to 11 plastic bottles, and also the heel, lining, and laces are made from recycled material.

'Our ultimate ambition is to eliminate virgin plastic from our supply chain,' said Adidas executive Eric Liedtke in a press statement.

In 2017 the company went further, launching in coincidence with World Oceans Day the limited edition of 50 pairs of the UltraBOOST Parley sneakers designed by Stella McCartney.

The only possible way to get a pair of those brand-new models was to take part in an Instagram competition, submitting a video that demonstrated their commitment to ending disposable plastic items.

Although the initiative regards the transformation of plastic waste in general and not specifically waste produced by the fashion industry, it's a sustainable innovation that seems to be appreciated by all the environmental critics, but still there are no information about the entire recyclability of the shoes after its use.

CASE STUDY 3

Imagine a shirt that after years of use could throw simply on the compost and let it decompose among the vegetables scraps, so that one day it will be part of a fertile soil to help grow new raw materials.

This would be a great step into circular economy, and this is the idea behind F-ABRIC, a range of materials developed by the Swiss company Freitag.

The brothers Markus and Daniel Freitag stared in 1993 what would be now called start-up in Zurich, with a strong design identity and a clear recycle aim. They were making bags and accessories out of old track tarpaulins and car's belt and they grew rapidly, selling their products worldwide, and having their bags awarded for the design and selected for important exhibitions at MoMa.

During the last 5 years they decided to go further in their ecological vision, challenging themselves in procuring sustainable work wear for their 150-strong workforce and applying the lifestyle they were promoting also in the clothing field.

Freitag's owners were disappointed by the fabrics on offer: natural fibers like cotton will compost over time, synthetic fibers like polyester won't, and natural fibers are often blended with synthetic. Moreover, the seaming and the sewing goods make the recyclability of the clothes harder.

So, they developed their own F-ABRIC line for man and woman, 100% compostable material from broken twill to make trousers, to a jersey fabric for t-shirts. It consists in basic clothes for casual wearing, extremely solid, made with a special combination of vegetal fibers grown, produced, and assembled in Europe. The company has also patented the design for buttons that can be screwed off and reused, in order to close perfectly the loop, without loosing the hard-wearing.

'The whole biodegradation process needs certain conditions. So, it won't disappear while you are wearing it nor in your washing machine', says one of the founders, Daniel Freitag. In the compost bin this workwear would broken down completely within three months, but of course there are industrial composting facilities to take care of this process.

In the website Freitag gives many information about the raw material, the labor condition, the caring tips and the end-life of their F-ABRIC piece of clothes.

Surely this is an alternative approach to fashion waste, but it cannot be a discharge to massive consumption.

It is for an interesting initiative that give to design an essential role for the waste transformation, and it goes in the direction of Cradle to Cradle design Theory, but still many critical points have to be solved, such dying and printing processes.

SYSTEMATIC APPROACH VS GREEN WASHING

So far, we analyzed the fashion waste transformation through the material perspective and the brands' approach. But what is it exactly the role of the designer in this system? Concerning H&M case, the sustainable change looks to be driven by a consumer desire and expectation towards the brand. In the Conscious Collection the design is marginal, whereas it's given more importance to the fabric used and to the informational attributes. It represents the stereotype of an out-of-trends fashion that will last because of its quality and classy design.

The design of the Adidas x Parley is extremely linked to the cause and it is part of the brand policy. The product is very conceptual, its lines and colors suggest the history of its raw-material and its 3D production. From the engineering process to the promoting campaign, everything is coherently designed, and the challenge to make trash appealing is perfectly passed.

The waste transformation is part of the Freitag's DNA. The F-ABRIC collection is designed for the purpose to be destroyed after the use. The patterns, the cuts, the buttons, the colors are perfectly designed to permit the process and to give a unique, original and evergreen outlook.

This is the reason why the role of the designer will be more and more an undeniable push for the brand when it comes to initiatives in a 'systematic approach' to sustainability rather than 'green washing'.

Lizzie Harrison of Sustain RCA, a research hub within the Royal College of Art of London, says: 'Up to this point, it's fair to say that most of the fashion industry has been directed by compliance rather than innovation. So, they have done what they have had to do rather than taking sustainability as a springboard to do something very exciting.' She reminds that sustainability must be sitting in the design department, because that would represent a real challenge in terms of bringing sustainable innovation into the heart of an organization.

Nowadays the ability to recycle the image of a waste-transformed fashion product is an open challenge for the contemporary design.

REFERENCES

Context Analysis

[1] Ricchetti, M. (2017), Neomateriali Nell'economia Circolare. Milano: Edizioni Ambiente, p. 239.

[2] Valuing Our Clothes: The Cost of UK Fashion (2017), [pdf] WRAP, p.54. Available at: http://www.wrap.org.uk/sustainable-textiles/valuing-our-clothes%20

[3] Being wise with waste (2010), [pdf] p.20. Available at: https://publications.europa.eu/en/publication-detail/-/publication/882ba217-fd06-4b65-8d72-8a793d99d9bd/language-en

[4] Tartaglione, C. and Corradini, S. (2013), Il fine vita dei prodotti nel sistema moda. [ebook] Roma. Available at: https://www.slideshare.net/AresDuezero/il-fine-vita-dei-prodotti-moda

[5] The Balance (2018), I:CO Helps the Fashion Industry Close the Loop on Recycling. [online] Available at: https://www.thebalance.com/i-co-provides-fashion-recycling-options-2877813 [Accessed 21 Jan. 2018].

[6] Strijbos, B. (2018), Global fashion industry statistics - International apparel. [online] Fashionunited.com. Available at: https://fashionunited.com/global-fashion-industry-statistics [Accessed 21 Jan. 2018].

[7] Luxuryistohavesimplethings.com (2018), Elementum – Luxury is to have simple things. [online] Available at: http://luxuryistohavesimplethings.com/ [Accessed 21 Jan. 2018].

[8] Progetto Quid (2018), Home. [online] Available at: http://progettoquid.it/ [Accessed 21 Jan. 2018].

[9] Sampleness (2018), [online] Available at: http://www.sampleness.com/ [Accessed 21 Jan. 2018].

[10] PreLoved (2018), PreLoved [online] available at: https://getpreloved.com/ [Accessed 21 Jan. 2018].

[11] Makeuse.nz (2018), Make/use: A modular system for zero-waste fashion [online] available at: https://makeuse.nz/ [Accessed 21 Jan. 2018].

[12] Ico-spirit.com (2018), I:CO [online] available at: http://www.ico-spirit.com/ [Accessed 21 Jan. 2018].

Waste Transformation

[13] Richetti, M. (2017), Neomateriali nell'economia circolare Moda. Milano: Edizioni Ambiente, p. 239.

[14] Aquafil.com (2018), Aquafil – Il filo ECONYL® [online] available at: https://www.aquafil.com/it/sostenibilita/il-filo-econyl/ [Accessed 21 Jan. 2018]

[15] Econyl (2018), Econyl [online] available at: http://www.econyl.com/ [Accessed 21 Jan. 2018]

[16] Swedish Stockings (2018), Swedish Stockings | Shop Eco Friendly Pantyhose & Stockings [online] available at: https://en.swedishstockings.com/ [Accessed 21 Jan. 2018].

[17] Cardato.it (2018), English | Languages | Cardato [online] available at: http://www.cardato.it/en/ [Accessed 21 Jan. 2018].

[18] Filpucci.it (2018), Filpucci [online] available at: http://www.filpucci.it/ [Accessed 21 Jan. 2018].

[19] Trenery.co (2018), Trenery | Modern Women's Fashion & Men's Clothing. [online] Available at: https://www.trenery.co/ [Accessed 21 Jan. 2018].

[20] World Wildlife Fund (2018), The Impact of a Cotton T-Shirt | Stories | WWF. [online] Available at: https://www.worldwildlife.org/stories/the-impact-of-a-cotton-t-shirt [Accessed 21 Jan. 2018].

[21] Wasatex.eu (2018), Home [online] available at: http://www.wasatex.eu/it/ [Accessed 21 Jan. 2018].

[22] REMO (2018), Home [online] available at: http://remokey.com/ [Accessed 21 Jan. 2018].

[23] Bluelooporiginals.com (2018), Blueloop [online] available at: https://www.bluelooporiginals.com/story.php [Accessed 21 Jan. 2018].

[24] MUD Jeans (2018), MUD Jeans | Circular Denim & Ethical Esthetics [online] available at: http://www.mudjeans.eu/ [Accessed 21 Jan. 2018].

[25] Marchifildi.com (2018), Italian spinner creates cotton fibre from clothing offcuts | Marchi & Fildi SPA [online] available at: http://www.marchifildi.com/blog/italian-spinner-creates-cotton-fibre-from-clothing-offcuts/ [Accessed 21 Jan. 2018].

[26] Nowastenet.eu (2018), REMO – Join the recycle movement | NoWasteNet [online] available at: http://www.nowastenet.eu/website/remo-join-the-recycle-movement/ [Accessed 21 Jan. 2018].

Case Study 1

[27] Fashionrevolution.org (2018), Fashion Revolution. [online] Available at: http://fashionrevolution.org/ [Accessed 21 Jan. 2018].

[28] About.hm.com (2018), H&M group | Sustainability. [online] Available at: http://about.hm.com/en/sustainability.html [Accessed 21 Jan. 2018].

[29] The H&M Group Sustainability Report 2016 (2017) [online] Stockholm: H&M, p. 2. Available at: https://about.hm.com/content/dam/hmgroup/groupsite/documents/e n/CSR/reports/2016%20Sustainability%20Report/H&M%20group %20Sustainability%20Report%202016_en.pdf

[30] Worn Again (2018), Worn Again – Abundance. For Everyone. Forever... [online] Available at: http://wornagain.info/ [Accessed 21 Jan. 2018].

[31] Refinery29.com (2018), H&M Recycled Denim Collection – Green Fashion [online] available at: http://www.refinery29.com/2014/01/60894/hm-recycled-denim-collection [Accessed 21 Jan. 2018].

[32] Vimeo (2018), H&M Close the Loop [online] available at: https://vimeo.com/138181635 [Accessed 21 Jan. 2018].

[33] Bain, M. (2018), Is H&M misleading customers with all its talk of sustainability? [online] Quartz. Available at: https://qz.com/662031/is-hm-misleading-customers-with-all-its-talk-of-sustainability/ [Accessed 21 Jan. 2018].

Case Study 2

[34] Parley (2018), Parley for the Oceans [online] available at: http://www.parley.tv/#fortheoceans

[35] ADIDAS (2018), [online] Available at: http://www.adidas.com/us/parley

[36] Morby, A. (2018), Stella McCartney and Adidas unveil Parley Ultra Boost X trainers made from ocean plastic. [online] Dezeen. Available at: https://www.dezeen.com/2017/03/17/stella-mccartney-adidas-parley-ultra-boost-x-ocean-plastic-trainers-design-fashion/

[37] Vibes, J. (2018), Adidas Wants to Recycle Ocean Plastic to Use for it's Products [online] True Activist. Available at: http://www.trueactivist.com/adidas-wants-to-recycle-ocean-plastic-to-use-for-its-products/

Case Study 3

[38] FREITAG (2018), From Fibers to F-ABRIC. [online] Available at: https://www.freitag.ch/en/fabric

[39] Canapa Industriale (2018), Freitag lancia F-abric, nuovo tessuto biodegradabile con fibra di canapa e lino. [online] Available at: http://www.canapaindustriale.it/2014/09/30/freitag-lancia-f-abric-nuovo-tessuto-biodegradabile-con-fibra-di-canapa-e-lino/

[40] Zimmer, L. (2018), Freitag Launches 100 Percent Compostable Clothing Made From Plants. [online] Inhabitat.com. Available at: https://inhabitat.com/ecouterre/freitag-launches-100-percent-compostable-fabric-made-from-plants/

[41] Cradletocradle.com (2018), Cradle to Cradle | William McDonough & Michael Braungart: MBDC. [online] Available at: http://www.cradletocradle.com/

Conclusions

[42] Greenwashingindex.com (2018), About Greenwashing | Greenwashing Index. [online] Available at: http://greenwashingindex.com/about-greenwashing/

[43] Moulds, J. (2018), Can big brands catch up on sustainable fashion?. [online] the Guardian. Available at: https://www.theguardian.com/sustainable-business/sustainable-fashion blog/2015/mar/24/composting-clothes-sustainable-materials-biodegradable

Parivarthana – Waste Designed for Change

CENTRE FOR SOCIAL ACTION

Christ University, Hosur Road, Bengaluru, Karnataka, India

ABSTRACT

This is a case study highlighting the experience of CHRIST (Deemed to be University) in transforming trash into treasure. This paper aims to capture experiences of Centre for Social Action initiating action on campus to develop an integrated waste management system in order to encourage young people to be responsible citizens. Design by definition is the purpose or planning that exists behind an action, fact, or object. At Parivarthana, the Handmade Paper Recycling Unit of the University, efforts are made to convert the bulk waste into useful products by design, design that makes everyday life convenient and much more responsible. This paper attempts to propose Parivarthana as a model of social relevance more than one of business excellence. Nevertheless, the way forward deems it necessary to focus on profits with purpose strongly ingrained in the process, as a result of which we could present to the world a Model of Profitability for the Planet.

Keywords: *Solid waste management, Zero waste campus, Paper recycling, Products, Parivarthana, Sustainable environmental practices.*

INTRODUCTION TO PARIVARTHANA PROJECT

Parivarthana is an initiative of Christ University mainly tries to implement comprehensive waste management initiative within the campus. The case study mainly focuses on the recommendations to all the academies insertions and corporate to establish waste management initiatives for better sustainable development. Parivarthana is a model that tries to replicate waste management ideologies through different activities enforcing towards ensuring a zero waste campus. The goal of Parivarthana is to ensure sustainability through waste management by different mechanisms. The collection of paper waste is recycled into handmade products. The food waste is sorted-segregated and transformed into fuel as biogas and organic compost. The waste water or used water is also treated through the sewage treatment plant which is reused as water for gardening and flushing purposes. The case study focus on how our waste management process on campus emphasizes on providing a platform for paper recycling where waste paper is reshaped into useful products.

Parivarthana Works towards Providing

- A platform for product development from the waste generated within the campus
- New business model and opportunities, along with setting an exemplary model to recover new resources.
- Innovative reusable products by using new strategies to reduce the waste and dispose waste in a structured way.

OBJECTIVES

- To study how Parivarthana has contributed to the overall waste management of CHRIST.
- To reflect on the role and impact of Parivarthana- recycling unit in an academic institution.
- How Parivarthana has applied the principles of design in the process of product design

METHODOLOGY

The case study research methodology used in this study is to recommend sustainable waste management procedure for better product design. The study mainly explains through a model that can be replicated anywhere as a method of creating various products through waste management.

The two major components of the study are:

- Focus on product design and its sustainability.
- Keeping waste management at the base, and promote such platforms for product design which can be sustainable and useful products for institutions, families and communities.

RESULT AND DISCUSSION

The study was conducted with Parivarthana – Recycling Unit of Christ University to assess the evidence of success promoting sustainable hazard free environment. About 20,000 students and members of the faculty are sensitized and educated on solid waste management practices all through. Parivarthana works with two-pronged strategies, i.e. by recycling paper in-house and secondly by bridging the bulk generators of recyclables to the large recyclers that helps fulfill every organization's environmental responsibility. Christ University generates around 900-1000 kgs of waste everyday which includes both wet and dry waste; of which dry waste comprises of 80% and remaining 20% is wet waste. In the 80% of the dry waste, majority is paper waste derived from the written answer papers used by 18,000 students, which is a bulk waste. This waste is directed to Parivarthana for recycling. The other wastes are primarily segregated by students and members of the faculty who are being sensitized by CSA team and volunteers to involve and contribute to a clean and green environment, thus making university campus a Zero Waste Campus. It was at this point that we realized the design solution is in connecting the manufacturer with the waste, to create the right motivations to redesign the product. Ultimately, this meant designing the system before the product.

Our paper recycling centre started small. Using 'Reduce, Reuse and Recycle' as a guiding motto, Parivarthana has always aimed at developing the understanding with the students and the community about the value of waste and its proper usage though various products. We started with few products such as files and diary, from the evolution of Parivarthana being almost a decennial we have seen an increase in the different product designs that are been developed. Propagating the idea of waste as a resource, we have seen that from the recycling centre, utilizing its waste and converting them into beautiful hand-made, eco friendly and sustainable products. When a small waste product is broken down, it proceeds to go forward as an income and benefits the communities involved in this process.

Table 1: Products and its Area of Usage

Products	*Major Useable Area*
Pen stand	Office management,
Jewellery Box	Personal use, gifting purposes
Folders (Jute, hardboard, Black sheet)	Conferences, File management
Bags (Jute, paper)	House hold shopping
Photo frames, zig zag Photo Album and Photo album	House hold, gifting
Diary	Conferences, office uses, Gifting
Pen book	Conferences

In the table above, the innovativeness of design has been used by Parivarthana to produce products that are trendy, satisfying the need, eco-friendly, and sustainable.

Design sits at the heart of the challenge to create a circular economy. 100% of the product's environmental impact is "locked in" at the design stage, so understanding production cycles and reconfiguring them for maximum effectiveness is the main key. We do not simply substitute one material for another without understanding the consequences which will dilute the goals of Parivarthana.

Table 2: Economic Sustainable Model

Components	*Population*	*Process*	*Mode*
Reduce	Students and faculty	Orientation, Awareness	Street plays, Campaigns, Posters
Reuse	Students and faculty	Reuse Sewage treatment, alternative uses	Treatments and Molding
Recycle	Underprivileged women	Training and Capacity building	Workshops

In the above table we can see that there are 3 major components in waste management. To turn waste into attractive modes, we work in 2 phases:

1st Phase – Reduce and Reuse

In this phase we set out with organized effort in ensuring paper recycling practice. Paper is not a material that can be used with control. So reducing the use of paper in a vast university is a hustle, but the efforts that goes behind in recycling is a mean of reducing the amount of waste that we, you and I, produce each day. By using less we help conserve resources. Reduction is the first choice in reducing the waste stream. At this stage the Praytna team ensures that the student community is sensitized about proper usage of waste bins and assures that they are the primary waste segregators.

2nd Phase – Recycle

The marginalized women identified from urban slums given training and building their capacity to design new products and bring about new business models, thus helping them to earn a livelihood. Designing in this way is complex. Gone are the days of 'sustainable' or 'eco' design, when a simple change of material to a recycled alternative would give a project environmental credibility.

This effort needs to be led by innovative ideas and businesses models.. Now, however, the business model is changing and the economic imperative for recovery is growing stronger.

SUGGESTIONS AND RECOMMENDATION

Sustainable waste management model will be unique model for all the institutions, government industry and also for private sector to follow an efficient waste management practice to contribute to environment friendly initiatives. Parivarthana model of waste management is not only managing the waste but also trying to restore the waste into different products through effective product designing. It is an socio-economically sustainable and environment friendly model for inclusive integrated development. The waste that is generated through any population can be transformed into useful products. Reuse recycle and reduce mechanism has its own effective interventions to ensure that all the waste are not just waste but mass resource for effective economic development. Institutions can manage waste by themselves through promoting micro entrepreneurship among people through capacity building and training. Training and capacity building will promote people for effective contribution to waste management. The comprehensive combination of waste management and skill among product designing the technique will contribute to effective mechanism for sustainable waste management. Product design should be environment friendly and that can make good revenue for a particular population. The product designing is done considering the need of the market. By considering a family as market it should come up with useful products that a family can use. But on the other hand if the customers are from different institutions the products should be under the consideration of their need and interest. Such market analysis is also important for effective implication of this model. Such initiatives, interventions and mechanisms can easily resolve the issues of waste as a mess. Try to consider it as a resource and that have a wider range of scope for effective contribution to society for development and sustainability.

CONCLUSION

Parivarthana, the initiative of Christ University has been awarded by Rotary Club for comprehensive waste management initiative in the campus as well as in the slum community. The income generated through the recycling of waste is used for supporting the unit and thus promoting sustainable livelihood for marginalized women, which in turn maintains a clean and hygienic environment. The analysis on the result of case study conveys the green social work – social workers commitment to social and environmental justice and also mobilizing people to reclaim their resources and producing collective ways of meeting everyone's needs.

STORE ROOM
LEAF STORAGE

Kaveri

REFERENCES

[1] Zikmund, W., & Stanton, W. (1971), Recycling Solid Wastes: A Channels-of-Distribution Problem. *Journal of Marketing*, 35(3), 34-39. doi:10.2307/1249787

[2] Baetz, B., & Neebe, A. (1994), A Planning Model for the Development of Waste Material Recycling Programmes. *The Journal of the Operational Research Society*, 45(12), 1374-1384. doi:10.2307/2583931

[3] Folz, D. (1991), Recycling Program Design, Management, and Participation: A National Survey of Municipal Experience. *Public Administration Review*, 51(3), 222-231. doi:10.2307/976946

[4] Hershkowitz, A. (1998), In Defense of Recycling. *Social Research*, 65(1), 141-218. Retrieved from http://www.jstor.org/stable/40971254

[5] Briscoe, G. (1987), Recycling: What's in it for Libraries. *American Libraries*, 18(11), 954-956. Retrieved from http://www.jstor.org/stable/25631017

[6] Erickson, R. (1996). Paper – A Future or Not? Challenges in that Future. *The Commonwealth Forestry Review*, 75(2), 160-163. Retrieved from http://www.jstor.org/stable/42608286

[7] Paper and Allied Products (1975), *Journal (Water Pollution Control Federation)*, 47(6), 1402-1446. Retrieved from http://www.jstor.org/stable/25038866

[8] Sandhya, V. (1994), Managing Waste: Ecological, Economic and Social Dimensions. *Economic and Political Weekly*, 29(45/46), 2907-2911. Retrieved from http://www.jstor.org/stable/4401996

[9] Baetz, B., & Neebe, A. (1994), A Planning Model for the Development of Waste Material Recycling Programmes. *The Journal of the Operational Research Society*, 45(12), 1374-1384. doi:10.2307/2583931

[10] Srinivasan, D., & Unwin, J. (1995), Pulp and Paper Effluent Management. *Water Environment Research*, 67(4), 531-544. Retrieved from http://www.jstor.org/stable/25044593

[11] Darby, M. (1973), Paper Recycling and the Stock of Trees. *Journal of Political Economy*, 81(5), 1253-1255. Retrieved from http://www.jstor.org/stable/1830653

[12] Hershkowitz, A. (1998), In Defense of Recycling. *Social Research*, 65(1), 141-218. Retrieved from http://www.jstor.org/stable/40971254

Sustainability in the Fashion System as a Value

GIOVANNI MARIA CONTI
Department of Design, Politecnico di Milano, Milano, Italy
E-mail: giovanni.conti@polimi.it

ABSTRACT

This paper is focused on the sustainability design theme in relation to fashion and, specifically, how to create a service which gives 'value' to the product. This specific part was presented as part of the results of Sofia Aiello's Design for the Fashion System Master Degree thesis.

Starting, then, from a problem the goal is to educate consumers in alternative fashion product 'consumption'.

How can consumer awareness be raised? How can consumers be made aware of the quality of the garments they buy and wear?

How can the first steps towards sustainable fashion be made without falling into a facile utopian slogan trap?

Starting from the past, from ways of saving, conserving and looking after clothing to create a system which discourages consumers from throwing their clothes away and encourages them to create new bonds with these and build a history with them.

Responding to these questions and finding potential solutions to them required analysing the issue in depth, tracing an ideal fashion system development trajectory and describing its characteristics and action methods.

Overall, then, the main objectives of this paper are threefold in order to demonstrate that sustainable design in contemporary fashion is:

1. Necessary
2. Affordable
3. Possible

Keywords: *Service-design, Fashion, Clean process.*

A MATTER OF SUSTAINABILITY

The sustainability theme is a complex one. It cannot be reduced to simplistic terms and neither can it be solved quickly and easily.

What is it? What aspects of the industrial and design chain does it affect? When is a product sustainable? How do we recognise one when we come across it? When does a firm fulfil all sustainability requirements and when is it using this label inappropriately?

The best way to respond to these questions is by starting from some definitions:

'Sustainability is conserving life by means of environmental balance – human, animal, vegetation and planetary. A self-sufficient system is one which takes no more from the environment than it gives back, which does not exhaust resources and is self-sustainable. What is meant by sustainable design? In the clothing sector it means implementing non-polluting supply and production processes which do not use up planetary and human non-renewable resources.

It pre-supposes that garments can be reabsorbed into the environment once their life cycles are over. To date very few producers, and even fewer garments, fully satisfy the sustainability concept.'(1)

There are, however, various levels of sustainability, various definitions, that is, which overlap in everyday language to such an extent as to be considered synonyms. In actual fact every definition defines a specific attitude and sphere of competence. Applied to firms, for example, we can speak of fashion as:

- responsible when all design and manufacturing action takes account of all those involved in its various processes (economy, society, art, culture, environment, etc.);
- sustainable when it aims to safeguard its relationship with the environment and society;
- eco-sustainable when it hinges above all on respect for the environment;
- ethical when it takes account principally of social interest and the common good.

All this is summed up in the 'fashion taxonomy' graph.(2)

"When we talk of sustainability we are talking of three things: environmental sustainability, thus attention to the way the environment is affected, modified or managed by textile manufacturing in particular.

There is also a social component involving people who have something to do with fashion or knitwear products, thus principally the manufacturing phase in which the social problem risk is high. History has taught us this: Industrial Revolution Manchester was certainly not a place in which workers' rights were respected and the same is true of Bangladesh where the Rama Plaza tragedy prompted profound thinking on sustainability for people as workers.

But people can also be involved in their capacity as consumers and it is thus also end consumer sustainability.

The third pillar on which sustainability is based is certainly economic considerations. There is no point in doing something which respects people and respects the environment but has absolutely no economic outlet whatsoever and thus, speaking of clothing, has no appeal and is not attractive enough to be bought. So the three pillars are the environment, society and the economy. This is a good definition of sustainability.(3)

For the purposes of greater clarity, then, we must turn all our attention to a company model designed to achieve the 'responsible system' label. If, in the past, the fashion system was an exponent of socio-economic change it should be expected at this juncture, too, to be able to do a great deal to shift awareness and change direction.

Being conscious and careful designers means looking in all directions, among other things, and keeping up-to-date on global events without ever forgetting about one's own backyard.

What point is Italian fashion at? What can we expect from the near future? How is it positioned sustainability-wise?

Italian fashion's worldwide position is an excellent one and it communicates powerful lifestyle, culture, tradition and quality messages. What seems normal to Italians is perceived as uniqueness, style and sophistication to international fashion. The pret-à-porter and accessory sectors have experienced moments of international magnificence and recognition. Saying that a product is Italian automatically guarantees excellence and adds value thanks to a collective imagination whole which links the (appropriately named) 'Bel Paese' to thoughts of the Dolce Vita.

'In a sector which is moving in the direction of broad spectrum change, our far-sightedness and the management quality of our strategy has enabled us to perform better than our competitors and achieve exceptional results in both operational and financial terms. In 2017, in an uncertain geo-political and macro-economic climate, we will continue to focus on organic growth in our fashion houses and value creation,'(4) commented François-Henri Pinault, Kering President and CEO (international luxury macro-group comprising Gucci) following on from such financial outcomes.

How is value created then? It is certainly a question of supplying consumers with clear guarantees and, at the same time, a history behind the product, showing a transparent manufacturing chain, integrating all of Italian culture, tradition, history, hand crafting and dreams into the product and, finally, taking something with a soul, a unique appeal to stores and homes.

This requires re-locating production, having a district chain and, at the same time, enhancing the local area and the lives of its inhabitants, transmitting skills and know-how to the young in such a way as to avoid important skills being lost and ensuring that artisan skills embrace modernity, novelty and future.

REDUCING CONSUMPTION AND INCENTIVISING THE ECONOMY

For a designer it is very important to follow 'clean' and responsible processes for the purposes of environmental and social sustainability.

What can make a difference, however, is undoubtedly a creative effort to gradually modify fashion's overall scenario. Today's designers must ask themselves: 'how can I bring innovation? How can I contribute to bringing about significant change?'

Reducing what we effectively buy but incentivizing the economy at the same time is the challenge we should be taking on in as near a future as possible. Some initiatives more than others field potential tools capable of incentivizing a discourse linked to unique clothing styles and conserving these over time.

The 'Custom' Phenomenon: New Creative and Commercial Challenges

Personalising or, in more international terms, 'customising' embraces a style similar to that of cars in which true enthusiasts start from a base vehicle identical to all the others and add parts, colours, decorations and amendments to it, to create a one-off piece in perfect accordance with individual tastes and expectations. Certain fashion houses have moved in this direction, especially sportswear producers, with the intention of stimulating new consumer interests. Customising takes place almost exclusively online with customers given the opportunity to modify the item of clothing or accessory chosen, in accordance with the options available, and visualise the result before buying.

This strategy accords a range of advantages:

- a more effective production line before moving onto product personalisation at a subsequent phase without risking a negative market response (the personalised product is effectively already sold and paid for);
- the opportunity to personalise products puts clients centre stage and brings them into the design process heightening client curiosity and prompting them to choose one brand rather than another;
- customised products constitute an added value linked to experience, novelty and uniqueness whose result is to raise product end price;
- for their owners customised products are one-off objects which highlight their

personalities and personal histories and thus difficult to substitute or, at least, have a longer term lifespan.

The NikeiD service launched by the ultra-well-known Nike sportswear brand ensures its clients a highly satisfying and complete personalisation service.

All this takes place on the brand's web platform with a full-blown dedicated personalisation phase. Consumers are guided through its phases and can decide to start from a range of starting points to achieve an end result (in this case, a pair of shoes):

- starting with a clean canvas – in this case all personalisable models are shown in white alone;
- starting from a material, choosing from mesh with graphics, plain mesh, suede or leather;
- starting from a colour, choosing from the most iconic brand colours;
- starting with an innovation, choosing specific characteristics for their shoes from technologies such as Nike Free, Lunarlon, Nike Air and Flyknit.

The 'Sharing' Phenomenon: The Development of a Different Economy

It is called the 'sharing economy' and put forward as a new economic model capable of responding to the challenges of the crisis and promoting more responsible consumption based on re-use rather than purchase and access rather than ownership. The 'sharing economy' concept has a long tradition, above all in Italy, ranging from mutual societies to co-operatives and social enterprise.(5)

The base concept is a little like that of libraries: using something we need or like and paying only for the 'rental' period required. It is thus that the commercial reality of the sharing economy, experienced especially in the technological context, were born: from cars to things to knowledge. Everything can be shared, from an ownership perspective, potentially infinitely but in practice only virtually.

Sharing economy models have three characteristics in common:

1. a sharing factor thanks to which skills or resources are shared on the basis of their presumed advantageous nature. Services function and are activated when consumers understand the potential for benefits of any sort, financial, social, experiential or otherwise. Sharing links in ideally with the concept of community, which is inevitably formed in this type of economy;
2. a horizontal relationship between people and organisations (there are no longer differences between financiers, producers and consumers);

3. a technological platform which enables the bonds between service users to be developed and maintained also thanks to the digital reputation which is shaped. Specifically in relation to the platform concept, it should be said that service provision, in this case, is performed directly by those involved as those who own the goods. In this respect the technological factor should not be forgotten as the fulcrum of the whole economic model as it is this which cancels out geographical distance and allows people who do not know each other to meet.

The presumed benefits of a sharing economy are, first and foremost, social wellbeing, responsible consumption, saving and waste reduction. What moves into second place with these new models, is the use of money and ownership purchase.

Today the sharing economy is starting to move into the fashion world, too. Specifically, the founding principle of sharing activities, in this case, relates to a concept which consumers are already familiar with: sharing clothes with friends. Today, however, the friendship sphere has widened to encompass full-blown online networks. Thanks to specific platforms, in fact, it is possible to exchange, rent or share clothing with other users. Responding to economic crisis, cutting back on waste, reducing individual costs: these are the objectives of such platforms. The Guardian newspaper has argued that the new fashion world 'must have' is web sharing sites. The data supports this notion: in 2013 spending in Italy on buying clothes or shoes fell 6.7% while online shopping increased 60% on platforms such as Zalando.

Furthermore, the Coop 2014 reports indicate that 21% of Italians are willing to share clothing online (more than Germany, France and Great Britain). The founder of collaboriamo.org, Marta Mainieri, who shares this concept, has argued: "The time to share has come. With crisis and the help of new technologies, collaborative consumption is gaining ground [...]. Sharing means making full use of goods which can be ceded temporarily or permanently and, in the latter case, we are talking of re-use. Money may or may not change hands but the main currency is trust. Individual user reputations within the community are fundamental and sites are equipping themselves with ad hoc insurance packages".

DESIGNING TO LAST

Thanks to technology and ongoing research, a great many dirt and crease resistant fabrics and finishes have been developed as well as home appliances and washing products capable of washing clothing at low temperatures.

The advent of the sharing economy is especially interesting in the context of a panorama in which sharing seems an effective way of maximizing effectiveness and yield.

'In the upper echelons of fashion, on the other hand, a trend shared by all the most important brand names is customer service improvement. Client assistance is a very delicate moment in which firms truly risk losing their fondest clients, clients who have been loyal for years. All it takes is a less polite word from an operator or an absent reply to a problem and clients do an about turn and disappear. So in a market in which competition is at its most intense, a top quality assistance service is a strategic key to retaining client loyalty and extending one's market share. The most important innovations have been on the 'emergency assistance' front activated when a leather bag gets dirty or an over-used foulard loses its original color. Until recently the large brands used external laboratory services for repairs or simply recommended trusted tailors and shoe repairers. But now they prefer to do it in-house and products are repaired by the same people who made them.'(6)

The Circular Economy

In addition to looking after and repairing garments it is also important to understand how to avoid wasting limited resources and using those in excess.

This is the task of firms working in the circular economy, an economy which has been gaining ground lately and is juxtaposed to simply recycling objects thrown away. Bringing this type of economic system into the fashion sector is much more important than in other sectors. Recycling textiles is very time consuming and expensive in terms of energy and financial resources. By contrast, in the circular economy profit and value is generated by reusing what already exists, limiting production and extending product – in this case clothing – life cycles.

There are three business models linked to the circular economy:

- circular, in which the purpose is 'close the circle';
- servization, whose purpose is to attach more importance to practicability than ownership;
- sufficiency, whose purpose is to eliminate waste upstream.

The circular model starts from the assumption that what is waste for someone may be a resource for someone else. It is thus a model which encourages reuse of goods. Examples are the second-hand goods market and the swapping trend.

A Swedish brand, Filippa K, is promoting the circular model for its own company with clients bringing back clothing they are no longer using receiving discounts on further purchases. In this way clients do not throw away garments still in a good condition and the brand earns profits twice on a single item.

The 'servization' model, on the other hand, aims to strengthen the network of services linked to repairing, renting and lending, just like sharing related applications.

In this case greater importance is accorded to an item's function than ownership of it as such. The priority is wearing it rather than having it hung up in the wardrobe.

The 'pay for service only' formula is fairly new in the fashion field while it is well established in other fields (car sharing, housing). An example of service linked to the fashion world is La Tote which enables users, on payment of a set monthly fee, to receive a monthly box of clothes which they can choose to wear repeatedly and then return at the end of the month or buy them.

The 'sufficiency' model, on the other hand, aims to use all available resources as efficiently as possible. This model is characterised by two different and well-defined trends:

- demand management (what Zara does – producing only what clients respond positively to in order to avoid wasting resources in failing or excess production);
- co-creation of products with end users.

According to research, implementing a circular economy in the near future could be a winning strategy. It is estimated that it might generate revenues of 1.8 trillion Euros in Europe alone by 2030.

THE NEED.LE PROJECT

Need.le is part of the results of Sofia Aiello's Design for the Fashion System Master Degree thesis and the processes is based on the sharing economy linked service panorama, born and disseminated on web platforms.

Need.le's sphere is an everyday use one fulfilling basic needs (everyday clothing maintenance) and special functions requiring more specialized professionalism (restyling, clothing redesign, etc.).

Today the collective tendency is to throw away what is longer of use or worn out or which we simply no longer like in stylistic terms. The potential for buying at ultra-low prices and in ultra-rapid time frames has led to overflowing wardrobes, shops and also personal tastes. We are incapable of identifying a style, clothing quality and its real value. In addition to economic and social factors, the critical environmental factor is not to be overlooked.

The Need.le web platform was set up to offer a different solution to consumers from those currently available.

The functions proposed are sub-divided into two phases: 'ordinary repairs' and re-shaping'.

The first relates to all garment maintenance work: hems, zips, patches, turning up collars and cuffs, etc.

The second phase is a matter of work designed to breathe new life into items which clients no longer like either in wearability or stylistic terms and involves rethinking garments as a whole and adapting them to the preferences of their owners. All the professional categories with the skills to satisfy such requests are involved: tailors, pattern makers, embroiderers.

The core of the Need.le service is making user garments perfectly wearable again. Whether the issue is wearability or style, a selected team of professionals works on finishing off garments from the starting point of client tastes or stylist suggestions.

Service functioning varies in accordance with the phase concerned: in the former, with simpler operations, users are involved to a greater extent while in the second phase it is professionals who are involved and these offer full-blown consultancy services in agreement with clients.

The benefits of Need.le services are multi-faceted: the potential for reducing clothing related waste, making garments last longer, the chance to increase the emotional bond between consumers and their clothes and an opportunity to use niche but currently unpopular skill resources.

The Need.le service is designed to look after its users' garments, offering them a repair and restyling service for clothes which have lost their appeal or are momentarily unusable. Users can request various services which Need.le proposes to complete as fully as possible, satisfying clients and possibly encouraging a new approach to clothing. It can thus be argued that Need.le must appear:

- stimulating, because users need to be encouraged and tempted to use services by means of ongoing creative stimuli;
- fun, because users must see the services offered as a game;
- pro-active as all actions are designed to achieve a higher purpose which clients must be aware of.

CONCLUSION

Research shows that responsible fashion system management is both possible and advantageous for firms attempting to win out in the long term. Intelligently done, the benefits for the environment and society can be tangible and vital and today we are in need of powerful changes and examples constituting a true change of direction for the fashion system. If fast fashion succeeded in this task (changing the system and our consumer habits), in its day, sustainability fashion can and must also succeed.

It is down to Italy to take on this challenge and the country is capable of giving an example and showing the world of fashion both commitment and results. Despite this it would be utopian to think of a rapid and painless revolution in this case, as cultures and behaviors, customs, rooted habits and education are involved. Time and constancy are thus fundamentally important ingredients in the success of this 'responsibility' enhancing project in the fashion field. Familiarising consumers with responsible and intelligent consumption, focusing on quality and not quantity, making a commitment to transparency and integrity in products: these are the challenges to take up and the objectives to be achieved in the coming years. Everything around us is unstoppable: defining new consumption models, lifestyles and economic and social conditions. And this cannot be ignored by a sector as vibrant as fashion.

The sharing economy is now real and design must play an active part in this change. The Need.le project is an example of the ways in which new entrepreneurial approaches can also be conceived of. In the modern world, fashion design is not simply studying aesthetic solutions and responding to visual concepts, but above all seeking out and finding concrete responses to both aesthetic and, above, well-being related needs. And conceiving of well-being without thinking of the environment around us is impossible today.

BIBLIOGRAPHY

AA.VV. Manifesto della Sostenibilità per la moda italiana, www.cameramoda.it

Brown, S. (2010), Eco Moda, Logos, Modena.

Conti, G.M., Poletti, F. & Rinaldi, C. (2016), Maglieria Made in Italy Knitwear. Stories and Talks, Silvana Editoriale, Milano.

Merlo, E. (2003), Moda italiana, Marsilio Editori, Venezia.

Dickson, A., Loker, S. & Eckman, M. (2009), Social Responsibility in the Global Apparel Industry, Fairchild Books, London.

Rinaldi, F.R. & Testa, S. (2013), L'impresa moda responsabile, Egea Milano.

UNI EN ISO 14040 (2006), Gestione ambientale, Valutazione del ciclo di vita, Principi e quadro di riferimento.

UNI EN ISO 14044 (2006), Valutazione del ciclo di vita, Definizione e Linee guida.

Vezzoli C. (200_), The Clothing Care Function, Final Report, Sushouse Project, Delft University of Technology.

REFERENCES

[1] Brown, S. (2010), Eco Moda, Logos, Modena, p. 15.

[2] Rinaldi, F.R. & Testa S. (2013), L'impresa moda responsabile, Egea Milano, p. 54.

[3] Conti, G.M., L'aspetto critico sulla moda sostenibile. Interview with Alberto Saccavini, in Conti, G.M., Poletti, F. & Rinaldi C. (2016), Maglieria Made in Italy Knitwear. Stories and Talks, Silvana Editoriale, Milano, p. 178.

[4] AA.VV., Il Sole 24 Ore (February 2017), http://www.ilsole24ore.com/art/moda/2017-02-10/gucci-traina-ricavi-kering-quarto-trimestre-vendite-brand-fiorentino-214percento-131257.shtml?uuid=AEBRCSS

[5] https://www.che-fare.com/che-cose-la-sharing-economy/

[6] http://www.bergamopost.it/tendenze/come-aziende-lusso-coccolano-i-propri-clienti/

Sustainability in Luxury Fashion in India
Adopting Sustainability as the Foundation for a Better Future

KOMPAL AGARWAL
Masters, Global Luxury Goods and Services Management, Politecnico di Milano, Italy
E-mail: kompal_agarwal@outlook.com

ABSTRACT

In the domain of manufacturing industries, the quantum of resources being utilized is far more than what is actually required, resulting in an excessive wastage of these resources. Sincere efforts must be employed to take the responsibility to not only recycle/ reuse these resources but to develop ways for their judicious use. This very philosophy to think about conserving resources leads to the coining of the terminology of 'Sustainability'. Sustainability is thus an idea that goods should be produced in a manner or way that do not use resources which cannot be replaced and do not damage the environment. In more generic terms, sustainability is the endurance of systems and processes, with an aim to conserve natural resource.

The Luxury Fashion Industry has long been working on the premise of excessive usage of resources with a view that there should not be any shortfall in the resources during the manufacture of their products. The textile industry makes use of a plethora of resources, including natural materials like cotton, wool, leather and fur, and artificial ones like polyester and viscose for most of its processes. Additionally, they use unaccounted amounts of water and energy, thereby creating an ecological imbalance which in turn has a direct impact on the planet, by quenching the limited natural resources.

The industry has been reluctant to update its historical technologies for years, largely due to the demand for low cost textiles fueled by the explosion of the fast-fashion industry. Although innovative and sustainable technologies exist, one of the major reasons preventing their large-scale commercialization is the lack of consumer interest in sustainable products and the willingness to pay for them. The brands hesitate to create sustainable products fearing the lack of a market, and need to create products that are commercially viable.

Luxury brands are particularly well-versed in creative designing, setting trends that have a halo effect, and enticing consumers by selling a dream. In turn, their business heavily relies on brand reputation and trust, therefore has a huge responsibility as well as potential to usher a new approach to sustainability. However, they face the challenge of aligning their products with consumer expectations, which in the case of sustainable products is still a grey area due to varying levels of consumer awareness and perceptions.

The need of the hour is to examine how the luxury fashion brands can create sustainable products that will interest their consumer, guided by the relevant trends in the near future.

This particular challenge on 'Sustainability Practices required to be adopted by the Fashion Luxury Brand Industries' has been undertaken as the research work to explore how a truly sustainable product can be created keeping the consumer in mind. The research work also chalks down the 'Roadmap of Sustainability in the Luxury Industry'. This would focus mainly on the Indian consumers considering the more versatile, high potential, emerging luxury market.

Keywords: *Resources, Carbon footprint, Sustainability, Pillars of sustainability, Socio-ecological impact, Fashion, Luxury, Polluting industry, Sweatshops, Threat of being exposed, Recycle, Reuse, Biodegradable, Upcycle, Transparency, Traceability, Luxury brands as influencers, Growing economy, Closet consumers, Developed markets, Critical success factors, Fad, Corporate social responsibilities, Sustainable development goals, Niche, Consumer trends, Sustainability as competitive advantage, Timeless.*

INTRODUCTION

'*Be a cause, not just a business. Have a higher mission.*' – Philip Kotler

Resources, the world over, as we all know, are vanishing at a very fast rate; the day is not very far when even water and air, the basic necessities of life, would cost a fortune. Luxury and Luxury Goods - A Distant Dream. We may continue to feign ignorance or be oblivious about it, but, resource crisis definitely is a real-time global issue. As humans, it is our moral and social responsibility to conserve the available resources, to its optimum possible extent, that are left with us, for the coming generations – to live the life of humans. In a span of just about next 10-20 years, vital REMs like silver, zinc, lead and copper will run out, which are the critical resources for making cars, electronics and gadgets of daily use like smartphones, T.V., computers etc. The phosphate mines, the source of phosphorous, which is critical for global food production are also under pressure. With the levels of water, biomass and fossil fuels on a very fast decline, and the increase in carbon footprints the world over; the discussions and awareness about the issues and importance of Sustainibility are now being given paramount consideration and are no longer just relegated as irrelevant issues. The concerns of the world welfare forums, or the UN annual meetings are thus, honestly, quite genuine towards bringing awareness about the philosophy of Sustainability.

'Sustainable development' is not a new concept. The term was coined by *The Brundtland Report*, published in 1987 by the United Nations World Commission on Environment and Development. From focusing on the three pillars of sustainability – Ecological, Economic and Social to incorporating the fourth pillar, Community, the term is evolving into a more inclusive concept. Still, so many people the world over, the businesses houses, Government organizations and authorities, decision makers of MNCs, etc., are unclear on the meaning of this terminology. Sustainability is thus, a holistic concept that imbibes every aspect of a business.

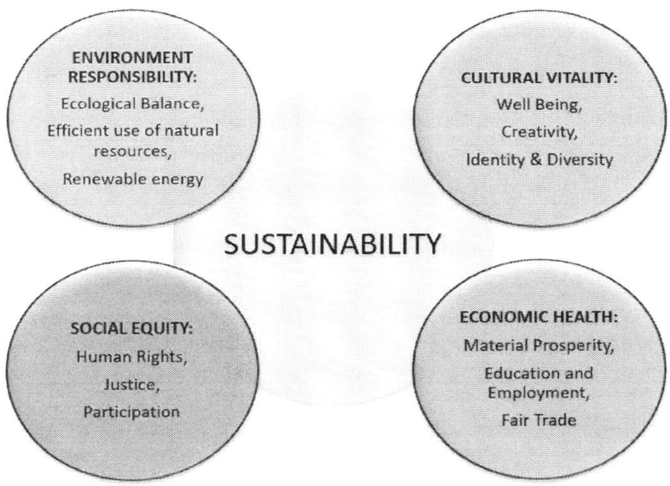

Figure 1: Four Pillars of Sustainability
(*Source:* The Brundtland Report, 1987)

As an ancient Indian tribal saying goes, '*We must replace back what we take to the mother Earth, what is not ours to keep.*' Putting it simply – sustainability is an attitude, it is a way of life that seeks not only to preserve and conserve all resources (land, labor, capital and community) that are available for its use, but also give back a greater amount than it took.

SOCIAL-ECOLOGICAL IMPACT OF THE FASHION AND LUXURY INDUSTRY

The Fashion and Apparel industry, being the second most polluting industry in the world, is only adding to the adversities by continuing its traditional practices of over production without being conscious towards the limitations of the natural resources. Fashion is a complicated business involving long and varied supply chains of procurement of raw materials like leather and textiles, production and eventually the shipping, retailing, usage and ultimately, the disposal of the garment. Eileen Fisher, American clothing designer known for her vision and contribution in the world of Sustainable Fashion, expresses her concern towards carbon footprint caused by the fashion industry [1]. Cotton, populates nearly 40% of our clothing, uses up nearly 10 per cent of agricultural chemicals while holding only 2.4 percent of the world's cropland space. It takes 5,000 gallons of water to manufacture just a T-shirt and a pair of jeans. This is as much as the daily water consumption of nearly 95 people in the urban India, drinking and utility purpose combined. Another popular belief is that, the leather and fur procured for footwear, bags, apparels and other accessories, primarily for the luxury sector, is a bi-product of the meat industry. Contrary to this, the cattle are bred to be killed. Most of the high-quality leather is made from calf hides, many a times, this is even extracted while the baby is in the cow's womb. Luxury fashion giants like Hermès, have been accused for keeping crocodiles in poor conditions in the past. These are just some of the examples of one of the dirtiest industries in the world. The malicious offshoot of the industry is not confined to the ecological impact alone. The 2013 incident of the Rana Plaza factory collapse, where in nearly 1,100 people were killed, left the world ablaze with the social impacts of the fashion industry. This has brought to light the poor, unsafe labor conditions in the prominent productions sites like Bangladesh, India, China, Thailand, etc. In many denim manufacturing factories, sandblasting technique is used to create distressed denims. While the safety instructions are provided to the companies, and many machine sandblasting techniques available, the process is still carried out manually in the sweatshops to save upon the cost. This is at the expense of the lives of these workers as it is resulting in high-profile silicosis epidemic in China since over a decade [2].

According to a recent Greenpeace report, an average person buys 60 per cent more items of clothing every year and keeps them for about half as long as they did 15 years ago. The clothing production therefore, has more than doubled in a span of last fifteen years. The production of such enormous volumes, with the progressively rising consumption levels is only adding to the stockpiles of landfill areas. As per a report by McKinsey & Company on '*Style that's Sustainable: A New Fashion Formula*',[3] it is estimated that: 'If 80 percent of the population of emerging economies were to achieve the same clothing-consumption levels as that of the Western world by 2025, and if the apparel industry does not become more environmentally efficient, then the environmental footprint of the apparel industry is expected to become much larger.'

With millions of people in the developing countries like China and India forming the enormous middle-class population base, and with the increase in the amount of HNWIs, the demand for clothing is going to increase significantly in the near future. Economically, at the same time, the purchasing power of the millennials has also increased remarkably, and this has given them the flexibility and latitude of choice. Even though the future for the fashion companies to continue with their old traditional practice of 'low-cost, high volumes production' may seem like an opportunity; it in fact poses a greater risk than foreseen. The fashion brands are thus at a threat of being exposed, because of the growing awareness about sustainability amongst the millennials and the generation – z, which is known to be much higher than the previous generations. With the rapidly changing lifestyles, there are higher expectations of the consumers from the manufacturing or production agencies.

Because of the crunch in the resources, the economy is now witnessing a transition. The production agencies, which earlier competed on the basis of – Prices, Productivity, Competencies, Labors, etc., are now competing on the basis of Resource Efficiencies, Reusability and their ability to Replace or Recycle the rare and expensive materials. Implementation of Sustainability Practices by the Fashion Brands, however, still remain to be incorporated by them in their processes.

Fashion brands are reluctant to invest in new technologies incorporating sustainability because the '*Sustainable Production Methods*' may cost more than that of their existing processes as perceived by them. They can however, tap the opportunities existing in Sustainable Production Methods to innovate and protect businesses from supply-chain shocks and reputation risks, leading to long term profits.

METHODOLOGY

The vicinity of study is of conceptual nature making use of secondary data.

The key objective of this research is to *Identify the Vitality of Sustainability in the Indian Luxury Sector for a Better Future.*

The paper is of descriptive nature. A descriptive study cannot conclusively ascertain answers to why. The secondary research data collection was carried to derive qualitative results and not quantitative results. Descriptive research is used to obtain information concerning the current status of the phenomena and to describe 'what exists' with respect to variables or conditions in a situation. This study relies primarily on deductive reasoning.

Furthermore, a lot of Blogs and Reviews over the much-hyped social websites such as Instagram, Twitter, You Tube, etc., were noted to validate the companies' communications as well as cross verified for the same information with the help of scholar articles.

The research has revealed some disturbing facts about the over consumption of resources which can only be controlled by a joint effort. However, the good news is that, even though the process might take a while longer, more efforts than expected, costs might be involved, but, sustainability being the megatrend that it is, is here to stay. And all these ingredients are only investments for long term benefits and better futures.

LUXURY, THE DRIVER OF TRANSFORMATION

The distribution of fashion has been described as a movement, a flow, or a trickle from one element of society to another. The most popular theory of distribution of fashion trends is the 'trickle-down' theory, where the diffusion of influence spreads from a central point – The Haute Couture to periphery – Mass Market or Value Market.

Because of the positional advantage in the luxury fashion hierarchy, the Luxury Brands, have a greater potential to harness sustainability as a business strategy, at the same time they also have a higher reputation at stake.

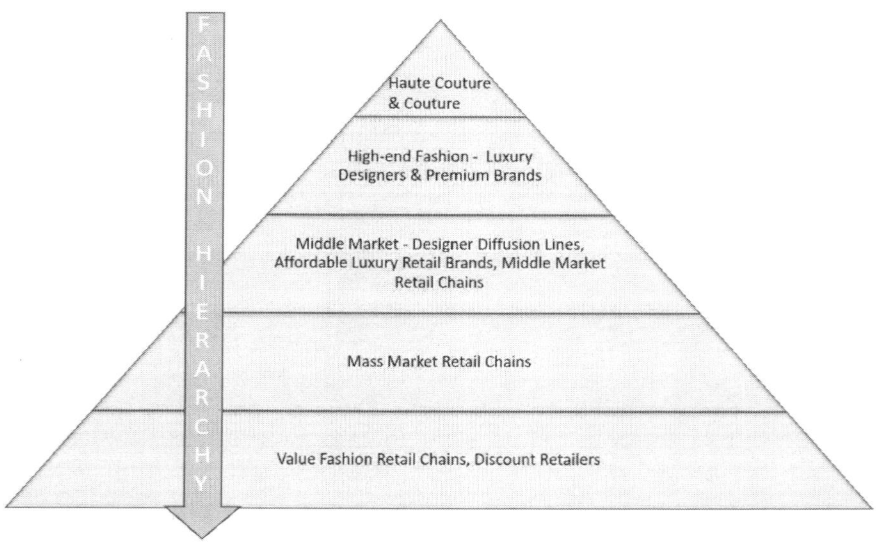

Figure 2: Fashion Hierarchy

On March 21st, 2017, (attended by me in person) The Prada Group launched an event, 'Shaping a Creative Future (SCF)'. The central idea of discussion that evening, was 'How to Design Sustainability through Innovation and Tradition'. The seminar not only catered to the industry's interest in sustainability, it also covered expert talks on customer's buying decisions driven by brand authenticity, history and provenance. Very thought-provoking questions were raised at the seminar such as:

- What are the meanings attributed to sustainability today?
- Can sustainability drive value creation and innovation within a business?
- How to create sustainable values through heritage and arts?
- How to move from greenwashing and build a truly sustainable business?
- What is the role of innovation and tradition in generating sustainable and social outcomes?

The magnitude of the event dedicated to the cause of sustainability showcased a clear picture, that the luxury industry is hard pressed and felt wanting in the domain of Sustainability. The brand CEOs, experts, visionaries, decision makers, designers, etc, were all in positivity to see a bright future for sustainable development. However, there were still concerns about the slow pace of the movement and inhibitions of the brands to adopt sustainability at their core [4].

A Sneak-Peek into Indian Luxury Market

Fondly addressed as the Golden Bird, India has always been the center of attraction for various forms of trade. There has been an age – old love affair between branded luxury and the nation of royalty. Brands such as Cartier, Rolls Royce and Louis Vuitton till date share their tales of fondness amongst the connoisseurs of luxury, the Maharajas and Nawabs of this country since the beginning of the '90s. The diverse art forms, rich, colorful heritage, handicrafts and textiles is what lures the designers and luxury brands to gain inspiration and to be able to compete in the land with a refine taste in luxury.

India is the second fastest growing economy in the world. It is seen as a huge potential market for luxury and addressed by many as having 'arrived'. With the changing scenarios in the developed countries such as the US, where consumers are now spending more on 'experiences' than on products, the fashion and retail brands are now looking at developing markets such as India and China to explore new possibilities of growth. With the population of 1.37 billion and 1.3 billion residents, the growth in disposable income has been 11.5 percent and 7.5 percent in China and India respectively. Compound Annual Growth Rate (CAGR) of India's retail market would be seeing an increase of 10 percent from US$ 641 billion in 2016 to US$ 1.6 trillion by 2026. B2B e-commerce in India is estimated to reach US$ 700 billion by 2020, while B2C is projected to be around US$ 26 billion. Escalating younger and aspirational middle class and a growing sense of 'brand consciousness' are steering the growth for luxury sector in India. Rise of e-commerce has also contributed to this factor along with increasing awareness and desire to satisfy the need to own and possess desired brands.[5]

With the fall back in the Chinese luxury as well as the retail scenario, India is seen as the most promising market by the luxury and retail brands. India's luxury sector is expected to grow by about 30 to 35 per cent over the next three years – across categories such as fine dining, electronics, luxury travel, luxury personal care, fashion, and jewelry. Upon an interaction with Ms. Anna Zegna, the granddaughter of Ermenegildo Zegna at SCF, she expressed her disappointment at Ermenegildo Zegna, the Italian luxury suit-making brand's retreat from India in 1999, due to lack of appropriate environment and inability to crack the import duty code. Nevertheless, she says, the situation has changed now and India is a budding market for the luxury brands.

The ambiguity of the multifaceted Indian market, demands patience by these luxury brands because of the lack of suitable infrastructure, government policies on import goods, and understanding of the archetypal Indian consumer.

Despite the beaming future there are many challenges faced by the luxury brands to overcome this ambiguity of the Indian market. Two third of the Indian consumers are below the age of 30. Even though there is a growth in the HNWIs, there is an aspiring class of Closet Consumers. These are aspirational consumers but may not have the ability to afford luxury items. Also, when it comes to jewelry and clothing, this type of Indian buyer is still traditional in preference, price conscious and less brand aware of the many more options present in the country than there has ever been. Unlike China (where luxury re-entered only five years ago), India has various structural barriers. An article by Neha Bohra reads, import duties are high (20-150 per cent), foreign investment in luxury retail comes with strings attached-100 per cent FDI in both single and multi-brand retail that too requiring 30 per cent of local sourcing, a clause which luxury players find difficult to comply with. The lack of proper infrastructure in quality retail real estate adds to the difficulties. At present, luxury malls such as DLF Emporio Delhi, Palladium Mumbai, Quest Mall Kolakata, Bergamo Mall Chennai and UB City

Bengaluru are only some additions to platform the international luxury brands, but are not enough.

Still, giant players are hopeful on India. Brands such as Moet Hennessy launched its first 'Made in India' sparkling wine. In 2011, Chanel launched its 2012 Paris – Bombay Collection, Hermès launched its limited saree collection which became sensational worldwide.

This seemingly impermeable market is not mainstream like China, and has its own unique charisma. It is diverse and contradictory. Tapping the right kind of consumers require patience and deep understanding. Luxury brands cannot adopt the same strategies as in China to penetrate into India at a very fast pace. The head representative LVMH Asia, Tikka Singh says 'India is a long-term play, you can't expect short term results. India is a young market and it's the last big luxury frontier. But many brands in our industry have shied away and not committed enough investment.' With a radiant tradition and expertise in textiles, leather, personal care (Ayurveda) and jewelry India holds a great potential for growth. There is a prominent movement of Indian fashion designers being recognized globally. Designers like Ritu Kumar, Tarun Tahiliani and Sabyasachi have stores abroad and are highly appreciated. Hidesign, the brainchild of Dilip Kapur, is a premium leather Indian brand, Forest Essentials is taking Ayurvedic recipes into high-end personal care and Amrut is a delicious Indian single malt gone rave around the world. The royal heritage of fine dining and spas in India too is the perfect platform to seize opportunity by the high – end luxury hospitality and service sector. Not only hotels like Taj, Oberoi, ITC have all created a name for themselves internationally, in fact are worthy competitors to names such as The Claridges, and JW Marriot. French ambassador to India Jerome Bonnafont told in the 2008 luxury summit, 'because of lavish Indian weddings, media advertisements, maharajas and Bollywood stars, I feel the art of luxury is alive in India.' The key is to study and seize the opportunity while the brands still can. The major conglomerates such as Reliance Brand, Genesis Colors, DLF Franchises, etc., have contributed exponentially to the growth of the Indian luxury scenario.[6]

CONVERGENCE OF LUXURY AND SUSTAINABILITY

A study of the literature from leading experts suggests that the underlying qualities of Luxury and Sustainability are essentially similar. Historically luxury was the privilege of those who had money, taste and power. An augmentation in the consumer base has led to the growth and deviation in the true sense of luxury. The accessible mass-produced items, even if endorsed by luxury brands, cannot be qualified as luxury products.

A deeper analysis reveals Luxury and Sustainable Development converge: both focus on rarity and beauty. The essence of real luxury is to sell high quality, creative and rare objects with an image of good taste and elegance.[7]

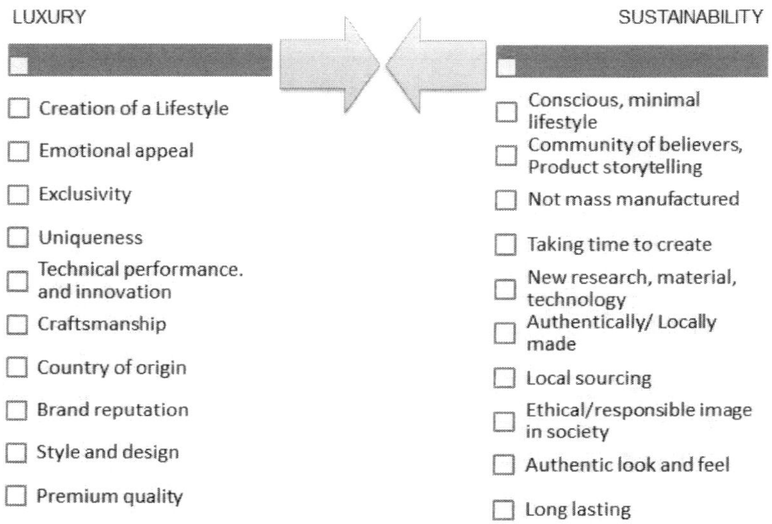

Figure 3: Luxury and Sustainable Development

Durability is at the heart of sustainable development as well as luxury. It is the enemy of the mass market industry or fast fashion trends observed popularly in brands like Zara, H&M, Forever 21, etc., which is based on planned obsolescence. On the contrary, luxury is the business of lasting worth. It thrives on the concept of high quality and timelessness. As per a report by The Guardian, sixty per cent of all Porsches produced are still being driven, plenty of which are from the '50s, '60s, and '70s, are still available for sale on the listings of sports cars [8]. Louis Vuitton provides after sales services to any genuine Louis Vuitton product, regardless of when it was bought. The same holds true for Ferrari: the Maranello mechanics will work on any old Ferrari, whatever its age. This is why there is a large aftermarket in the luxury business. The central idea behind this being the product you buy once and can be used forever.

Wolfgang Stelling, head of Strategic Business Development Concinno lists some of the Critical Success Factors (which makes a Luxury Brand what it is) being, factual and emotional superiority, and their uncompromising attitude. He also says that in order for the success of a luxury brand, assets such as rarity, scarcity and authenticity is what adds value to these brands to belong in the closed elite circle. Small production quantities, limited editions, selective distribution and exquisite materials make their products accessible to only a few people. It is very important that luxury brands remain honest in their communication to gain the customer loyalty. Another important point to remember here is that the luxury brands are personal. They enhance the customer's lifestyle and hence, it is crucial for these brands to be sensitive towards the customer's demands.

The need to be always on top of their game is also pushing the big Luxury Conglomerates such as the Kering Group to complete the loop. It is aiming for 95% traceability of its key raw materials by 2018 and 100% by 2025.[9] Under which, labels such as Stella McCartney, Gucci, Saint Laurent and Bottega Veneta are dedicated towards achieving their Sustainable Development and Integration Goals. The privileged positioning of the luxury brands, brings more opportunities with which comes greater responsibilities. These brands have a significant impact on sustainable consumption through their influence on the people around the world. Luxury brands promote concepts of quality, style and, ultimately, success. The scale and urgency of the sustainable consumption challenge urges all those who communicate widely, including iconic brands, to create a movement, an authentic understanding of quality, style and success, which includes respect for each other and the planet upon which we depend. In reality, the most successful and iconic brands, especially in the worlds of fashion and technology, do not so much respond to consumer demand as create and influence it. They do this in two ways: by 'editing' consumer choices through product design, distribution and other attributes over which consumers have no control; and by influencing the choices that consumers can make, such as how and when to use their products.

'Fashion in design fosters creativity and the exploration of new, previously untried solutions', notes design Professor Stuart Walker. He explains that sustainable design is neither a destination nor a fad, but a new paradigm within which fashion will move.

A recent work by WWF and others has demonstrated that consumption pattern, beginning from the way the products are bought, their utilization and final disposal – must be changed, if we are to stand a chance of combating climate change. For businesses, this does not mean reducing revenues from consumers, but offering them new types of value in less carbon – intensive ways. This can be achieved through a combination of intelligent design, appropriate messaging and practical support for consumers.[10]

Sustainability in India

Sustainable and environmentally friendly practices and psyches still continue to be part of the lifestyle and culture in India. The nation has both a culture of hoarding (in case something might come in useful), and thriftiness (re-use and hand-me-downs). 'It is not an uncommon sight in an Indian household to witness an old cloth being used as a duster', said a report of the India Economic Summit (IES). 'Things which have absolutely no value, such as old newspapers and books, or utensils, can be easily sold off to a scrap dealer to be re-used or re-cycled. Bucket baths, sun – drying clothes, and hand-washing dishes are other widespread, sustainable practices. Culturally, there is also an aversion to wasting food,' the report added – which has been based on data submitted at UN's High Level Political Forum from the Voluntary National Review Report on Implementation of Sustainable Development Goals.[11]

The economic progress in India is prominent in most places. The cities are becoming more advanced, transportation systems are booming, the people are better dressed and well fed, there are improvised schemes to face the global scenario. In spite of all this, as the human population is exploding, resources are shrinking. There are still many pockets in the country which have not been catered to India, is not only the growing hub of fashion and luxury consumer base, it is also one of the major producer and exporter to the international luxury brands in terms of raw materials, textiles, leather goods and even services. India's overall textile exports during 2015-16 stood at US$ 40 billion. The currently estimated US$ 120 billion Indian Textile Industry is expected

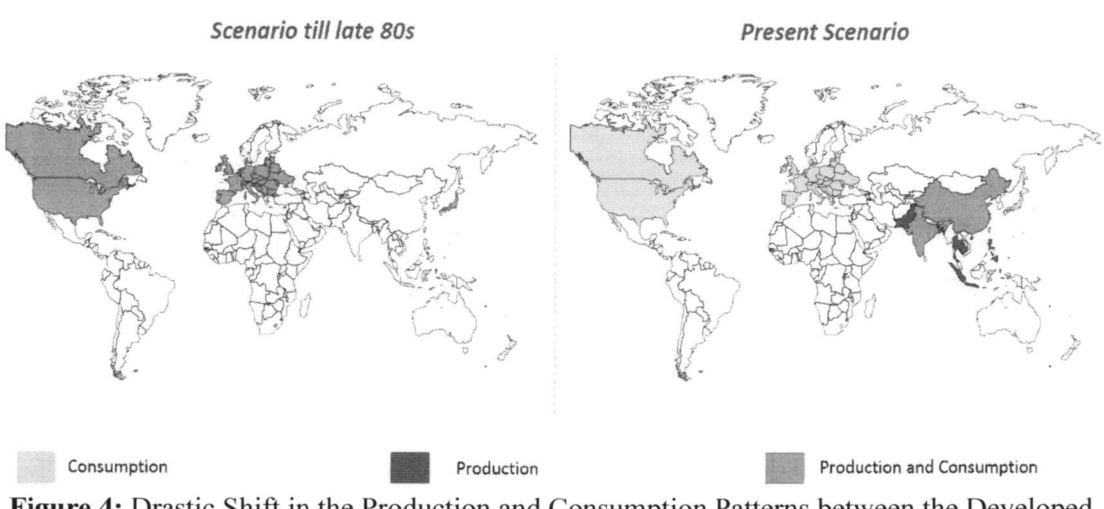

Figure 4: Drastic Shift in the Production and Consumption Patterns between the Developed and Developing Economies

to reach US$ 230 billion by 2020.[12] The exports of leather and leather products over the past decade has increased from US$ 2494 to US$3400. A report by FICCI shows the drastic shift in the production and consumption patterns between the developed and developing economies. Below is an image to give an idea of the same.[13]

The green area on the right (Present Scenario), indicates that these countries are victims of both production as well as consumption, which explains the instability in trends of this region. There is a continual demand from the developed markets, and increasing demand from the growing economies. Here, there is a limit to the site of production, resulting in further confinement of resource limitation. This is an important enough reason for the luxury brands to focus on achieving sustainability in their supply chains, recycling and upcycling of the products, their 100% biodegradability, longevity of the product life and be committed to after sales services.

With the developed countries like the U.S. and the U.K. seeing trends such as slow fashion, minimalism and experiential luxury rather than indulging into obnoxious shopping patterns, the fashion retail and luxury companies are turning their focuses towards India and China, the emerging Asian super powers for benefits. With the rise in consumption and over production levels, it is only a matter of time when this trend would also lead to its saturation and eventually, a decline. Which is why, it is important for the Indian Fashion and Luxury

Industry as well as the Consumers to make the most out of the learnings from the matured markets.

Upon the introduction of Corporate Social Responsibilities (CSRs) in India's new Companies Act 2013, the sensitive topics of discussions such as labor conditions, material procurement, women rights and safety in workspaces, etc., has started gaining more attention and action implementation. This shows that the subject of sustainability, though novel, has been seeing slow advancement and support from various National as well as International Platforms.

India is one of the 193 United Nations member states to adopt Sustainable Development Goals (SDG) and has committed itself as a stakeholder to meet the 2030 agenda for sustainable development. What is to be seen here is, if India will be able to do justice to these 17 goals or face a slack similar to the 2015, Millennium Development Goals (MDG). Though SGNs being the successor of MDGs, are much more comprehensive, attracting more focus and efforts by the Government of India.[14]

Fashion for Sustainability

The Indian Fashion Luxury and Textile Industry is not far behind to try its hands at this untapped philosophy of sustainability in terms of – brand values, design innovations, prototyping, re-evaluating their raw material procurements and traceability, possibilities of 100% recycling of finished products, better infrastructures and machineries, type of communication to the consumers, etc. Recently, at the *Lakme Fashion Week 2017*, Mumbai, what was formerly developed as Textiles and Handlooms Day each year to promote Indian artisans, got renamed as 'Sustainable Fashion Day' with its Winter

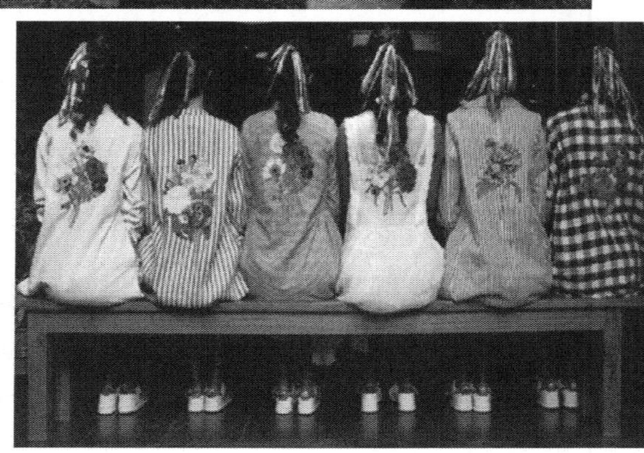

Festive 2017 edition. Anavila Misra, young talented fashion designer, showcased her romanticized collection of black and greys with the edging sheen using handwoven cotton, silk, linen and wool. This was a joint effort paired with craftsmen from the Paramparik Karigar group, which is a 20-year-old crafts sustenance body.[15]

One very popular example of an upcycled designer label is 'Doodlage' created by Kriti Tula, Paras Arora and Vaibhav Kapoor. The entire label is dedicated to the concept of upcycling and labelling. From swatches of fabric, old pair of denims, tested pieces and vintage garments, to a completely brand-new pair of clothing, the USP of this label is its eco-friendly, no waste philosophy. *Péro* by Aneeth Arora is a brand that believes in worker ethics and women empowerment. They work with handloom textiles and have a no synthetics policy. Where every collection is recycled and reproduced to beautiful patchwork pieces. They also encourage the consumers to recycle their existing garments.

There are many other niche fashion brands which are trying to contribute towards ethical sensibilities. For instance, *NoNasties*, whose mission is to eradicate farmer suicides in the cotton farm industry. This fair trade certified label promotes minimalistic outlook and has a strict policy of 100% organic textiles. Similar to this, there are brands such as *Upasana* and *Bhusattva* which are the leading and truest sustainable fashion brands on India. *DoYouSpeakGreen* is another very good example of an eco-friendly brand which is dedicated towards making fashionable yet 100% biodegradable garments and are already exporters to many leading international brands.

The game of the luxury footwear sector in India is also not far behind. A recently establish fashion luxury label, *Rungg*, is experimenting in different ways to be ahead of the curve in its global luxury scheme. This ethical, vegan brand is already very well known for its beautifully hand-embroidered shoes and strongly believes in empowering women.

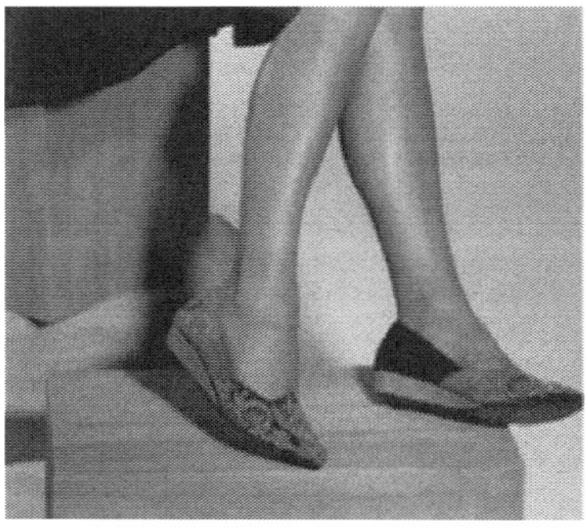

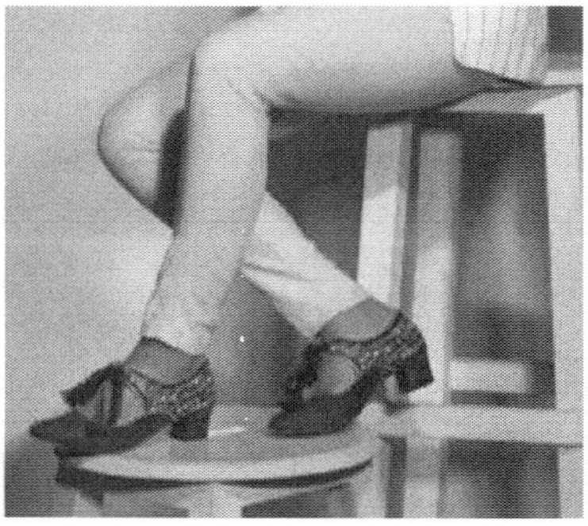

Paving the way for these niche brands however, we have labels by designers such as Anita Dongre who relaunched her label 'Grassroot Anita Dongre', to be in line with the philosophy – Revive Sustain Empower. An article by Tallulah D'Silva on Environmentally Write reads,

> *'think Indian fabric or Indian ready to wear garments and while Khadi with its patriotic flavor does find favor both locally and globally, the image of quintessential India in a brand that instantly pops up is none other than Fabindia. Urban India will surely vouch for its popularity.'*

These ethical yet modern, conscious fashion and luxury brands that are trying to revive the Indian heritage have taken the first bold steps towards sustainability. However, this would not be enough. India, even though shares less than 2 percent in luxury cohort, has a long way to go and learn from the developed markets.

Takeaways from the Global Scenario

Changing Trends

Below are some highlights of the upcoming consumer trends, supported by the data gathered in September 2017 MICAM organized by WGSN, Milano, Italy:

- **An Overdose of Fast-Fashion:** Statistics indicate that in 2002 sales of clothing were worth \$1 trillion, and rose to \$1.8 trillion in 2015. It is forecast to rise to \$2.1 trillion by 2025. This represents huge volumes of material - clothing production doubled from 2000 to 2014. Fast-fashion has long fueled a lifestyle of consumers buying trendy items in excess of their needs, only to dispose them after barely few wears.

  As re-cycling has its own limitation, ultimately, it is important to both close the loop and to slow down the rate that we consume by focusing on the clothes that are needed and re-thinking the systems used to supply them, taking in all stages from their design to their re-use or recycling.

  Maxine Beclat, co-founder of Zady expresses that consumers are reaching their limit. While the pleasure of cheap fashion is neurologically very real, consumers are equally experiencing the mental exhaustion from the accumulation of cheap clothing. The fashion system is broken and the consumer is hungry for change.
- **New Consumer Trends and Lifestyles:** The crucial changes of the last decade (intense development of emerging economies, the advent of globalization, the

spread of new information technologies, the process of aggregation of many large international groups, etc.), together with the economic crisis of 2008-2009, generated the birth of 'the new global consumer' in the market.

Consumers have come to appreciate sustainability and to look for ethical products as a benchmark for high quality and reliability. Such buying behavior was defined as ethical purchase behavior or ethical consumption by Harrison, Newholm and Shaw in 2005.

The consumers are increasingly becoming aware of the products they are buying. They are enquiring about thing like – country of origin of the luxury fashion products, where Made in Italy topped the chart of preference, followed by Swiss watches and German cars, the wash – care instructions, product lifespan whilst utility. A BCG study showed that the source of goods still remains a key issue, with around 80% of consumers claiming to verify the origin of the products purchased, especially in emerging countries. [16]

- **Creating Communities to Engage the New Consumer:** Luxury fashion brands should encourage positive feelings and moods that are commonly shared by customers, who become interconnected through the brand's aura. This action plan should shift the conversation from 'you' or 'me' to 'us', creating a collective feeling. Brands will then become an active part of the most recent phase of the 'democratization of luxury' that can be called 'humanization', in which the dialogue with clients and prospects will play a crucial role within an emotionally interconnected society.[17]

- **Technology and design Opportunities:** A senior manager interviewed by BCG and GFA in the Pulse report stated that the risk-averse attitude of companies to invest in new technologies and research will separate forerunners from the ones that get left behind. The role of research and development in a wider sense than just product development will increase in the future. The companies that are able to turn their company culture into innovative one, are the ones to shine in consumer's minds in the future. The challenges that our industry is facing cannot be beaten alone. We need collaboration and our competitors need to become our partners. The main competitive advantage of design brands and retailers is not in the materials we use, it's in the design. (Comments from a senior manager in the survey conducted by BCG and GFA, Pulse of the Fashion Industry, 2017) [18]

  Bio materials made from milk and mushrooms and other natural sources are the future of fashion and will be the norm by 2019. Ferragamo recently launched a collection made from Italian patented Orange Fiber which is created using citrus waste, with prints designed by the award-winning Mario Trimarchi. The brand describes the exciting development as 'a new fabric treated like the pages of an imaginary book on the colours of shadow at midday…demonstrating the vivid effects of light and shadow and freehand drawing to suggest clouds in motion and the wind scented with orange blossoms of the Mediterranean.' 'Biodegradable is definitely the new chic, looking "on trend" but with less impact on the environment' – Designer Mara Hoffman, spoke to Vogue this year about her shift to sustainability, beginning with her Spring/Summer 2017 collection, which featured better-for-the-planet textiles such as recycled spandex, tencel, organic linen, and organic Japanese cotton jacquards.

Using Sustainability as the Competitive Advantage:

The luxury brands face competition from not just the immediate competitors, but also the mass production brands in terms of higher sales as a factor of broader consumer reach. Since the research aims at studying the current and future trends and challenges of the Luxury Sustainability Environment, it is only apparent that a combination study of selected brands is done. The three brands namely, *Stella McCartney*, *Adidas* and *H&M* have been strategically selected to get necessary insights on the three principles which influence Innovation – Design Driven, Technology Push & The Market Pull. The case illustrations are formed after a thorough secondary study of the brands' Vision, Positioning, Sustainable Products, how the brands have overcome stereotypes about sustainability and the limitations on consumer perceptions.

MAJOR DRIVERS OF INNOVATION IN THE BUSINESS MODELS

- **Sustainability starts at the top:** The reason Stella McCartney's brand is so credible today, is because of years of consistent efforts towards improving every season. It starts with the top management really believing that it is the only way forward for a business.
- **Building a truly sustainable business takes time and a lot of research.** It took Stella McCartney 16 years to find fur and skin alternatives that were truly luxurious, but she showed that it can be done. If luxury brands are to move towards a sustainable future, they need to act yesterday, not tomorrow.
- **A business cannot sell on sustainability alone:** A study of Stella McCartney's brand positioning indicated how she focused on creating a distinct identity as a designer at the forefront, and implemented sustainability back-end, thus creating a truly sustainable luxury brand.
- **High quality is key:** As many reservations as we saw about the products, people who actually used the products had no complaints regarding the quality of the materials. People will pay the premium, but the product must exceed expectations.

- **No brand is perfect:** This is the perfect approach for a brand to begin its sustainability journey: to be humble and work harder with every collection.
- **Technology and Innovation can be a huge driver for sustainability:** Sportswear brands like Adidas have shown practical implications of using technology to create production efficiencies and be sustainable at the same time.
- **Collaborations can help scale-up sustainable technologies:** With its constant innovation in partnership with specialized companies like Parley and AMSilk, Adidas is working hard to scale up its sustainable product ranges.
- **Style, performance and sustainability can be mutually inclusive:** Adidas proved with the Parleys that a sustainable product can be high-performance and stylish at the same time. By positioning it at a higher price, they managed to capture the attention of the consumer.
- **Transparency in communication will go a long way in building trust:** With the Parley collection, it was noticed a sizeable number of comments about misinformation about the product. It was evident that consumers now want to know all the specifications of what they are paying for, especially when they are paying the premium. Adidas could look at this as a way to better communicate its efforts with consumers.
- **Reputational damage can possibly haunt a company for a long time:** Nike is still struggling with revealing holistic information, even though it is heralded on many sustainability indices as a brand that really turned its business around. We still see comments on social media about how its products are made in sweatshops, it still ranks low on transparency indices, information on its website is still vague, and it does not champion the cause in the way that Adidas does. Instead Adidas learnt from Nike's case, and acted ahead.
- **Sustainability can be desirable:** Bridging the gaps between design ideas and the material constraint to create fashionable, stylish garments, the H&M Conscious Exclusive, a capsule collection by the brand expressing its sustainable innovation, is the best example of glamorizing sustainability. Anne Sofie Johansson, Creative Director of H&M in a Vogue interview said, 'You can't believe the Bionic dress is made from old plastic bottles. It's a precious piece you can wear and cherish and save in your wardrobe. With the Conscious Exclusive Collections, we always try to find a new fabric or new technique. It's where we try to push the boundaries of what's possible with sustainable fabrics and show how beautiful the garments can be.'

- **The synergies of fast fashion and sustainability:** Broke stereotypes about positioning of fast fashion with a capsule collection, position to be seen as long lasting and coveted. They plan on scaling up these designs and already use Tencel used in previous conscious collections in their regular collections.
- **Capitalising on global reach to create consumer awareness:** H&M believes that sustainable fashion should be available for everyone. H&M has dedicated its sustainability strategies towards 'circular and renewal approach' acknowledging the fact that the population growth is going to continue to pull fast fashion business, but the brands (H&M) and the industry must look for new ways of working.
- **Brands have to start somewhere:** H&M's sustainability story is not so old however it is taking serious steps towards the paradigm shift. Being the world's biggest user of Better Cotton (source: better cotton initiative), H&M has commissioned a lifecycle assessment study to understand the impact of closing the loop recycling on cotton. It is also one of the founding partners of organic cotton accelerator foundation launched in 2016. It is also the world's second largest user of polyester in the world.
- **Changing consumer trends leads to transformation:** Market driven pull is driven by the needs of the market which can be fulfilled by incremental innovation. The conscious collection was created by observing the need for sustainability by H&M, which they have continuously innovated to make it better with time.

RESULTS AND CONCLUSION

Sustainability has always been the core component of the Indian culture. Its values and philosophies are deeply rooted to instances like the *yogic principle of aparigraha*,[11] which is a virtue of being non-attached to materialistic possessions, keeping only what is necessary at a certain stage of life. Then why is it that we as Indians, are getting carried away with the superficial ways of life? It is only obvious that we preserve our heritage and save the nation from its unhealthy spree of wastage of resources and energy. The companies need to look at innovative ways to work around conscious fashion, looking at the quality, durability, while lowering its ecological impact to create excellent designs and aesthetics in a luxury product. We as consumers need to educate ourselves about the eventuality of our purchase decisions upon not just the ecosystem but also our future generations. It is possible for us to increase the lifecycle of the garments we buy, by looking into their wash-care instructions and enquiring about the maintenance of the fabrics. We have the right to ask the retailers about the Country of Origin of the product and where it was manufactured. Sustainability, with its fourth pillar as community, is seeking for a joint effort from not just the industry experts, the decision makers, the government, but also the consumers who are entitled to question the efficiency of the brands and in turn drive the sustainable trend.

'*Sustainability is not a constraint, it's a field of opportunities at every level. It creates value in multiple ways – efficiency, innovations in processes and product development.*'

– François-Henri Pinault

To conclude, we believe that the four principles of sustainability, which are:

- Do old things in new ways
- Do new things in new ways
- Transform core business
- Build new model creation and differentiation

are going to take us far, seeing better futures with shared values and beliefs.

BIBLIOGRAPHY

[1] https://www.ecowatch.com/fast-fashion-is-the-second-dirtiest-industry-in-the-world-next-to-big--1882083445.html

[2] https://cleanclothes.org/resources/publications/Breathless

[3] Remy N., Speelman E., and Swartz S., Style that's Sustainable: A new fast fashion formula, McKinsey Company, 2016

[4] http://csr.pradagroup.com/en/event/shaping-a-creative-future/

[5. https://www.ibef.org/industry/retail-india.aspx

[6] http://iosrjournals.org/iosr-jbm/papers/Vol15-issue1/C01511827.pdf

[7] Kapferer J.,. All that Glitters is not Green: The challenge of sustainable luxury, The European Business Review, 2010. Available at http://www.theluxurystrategy.com/

[8] https://www.theguardian.com/technology/blog/2007/oct/15/thingstomakeyougohmm60o

[9] Crafting Tomorrow's Luxury 2025 Sustainability Strategy: Kering

[10] Bendell J. & Kleanthous A., Deeper Luxury, World Wildlife Fund Report. Available online: www.wwf.org.uk/deeperluxury

[11] https://www.weforum.org/agenda/2017/10/what-india-can-teach-the-world-about-sustainability/

[12] https://www.ibef.org/industry/textiles.aspx

[13] http://ficci.in/spdocument/20817/3-FICCI-TAG-2016-Whitepaper.pdf

[14] https://www.thebetterindia.com/89841/sustainable-development-goals-un-india-2030/

[15] http://www.vervemagazine.in/fashion-and-beauty/sustainable-fashion-day-2-of-lakme-fashion-week-winterfestive-2017

[16] BCG and GFA, Pulse of the Fashion Industry, 2017.

[17] Pittard V., Luxury consumption and sustainability, Cattedra Trade and Retail Marketing, 2015/2016. Available at: http://tesi.eprints.luiss.it/16504/1/659241.pdf

[18] Pulse of the Fashion Industry, Copenhagen Fashion Summit, 2017. https://www.copenhagenfashionsummit.com/

Role of Marketer in Moulding Consumer Buying Behaviour in Favour of Waste Management

PRAGATI SINHA

Assistant Professor, Fashion Department, MIT Institute of Design, Pune, India

E-mail: pragatisinha@mitid.edu.in

ABSTRACT

Consumer behaviour analysis involves issues like perception, comparative study, information search, attitudes, beliefs, decision making and categorization. Consumer behaviour is adaptive in nature: Consumers adapt to situations that surround them and they tend to get inclined by external forces. The major types of external forces include culture, subculture, social class, family, reference groups and friends, external conditions and marketing environment. Consumer spending in India is undergoing a reform and according to a report published by BCG in March, the consumer spending in India is expected to triple in the next decade. India is set to become the third largest consumer economy by 2025, trailing only the US and China, fuelled by an increase in consumption levels, changes in consumer behaviour and spending patterns. On the other side, India is getting choked with garbage disposal. Waste management that is one of the most serious issues that plagues India is a direct resultant of rising consumption. While experts are already implementing effective measures in waste management and by social workers to educate people regarding recycle and upscale of all forms of waste, the need to address this issue from a different perspective is worth a consideration. This paper calls to invoke the need to address the issue of waste management from the point of origin. The paper includes relevant case studies of how consumer buying behaviour is influenced by marketers. The author shares an affiliation with Indian fashion retail industry and presents an analysis of consumer sentiments about effectiveness of aggressive marketing and promotion of recycled and sustainable clothing. The aim of this paper is to highlight the pertinent role that businesses and their marketing verticals can play in reshaping consumer culture and redirecting consumer spending towards purchase of recycled, upscaled and sustainable products.

Keywords: *Consumer behaviour, Marketing and consumer culture, Business economics and waste minimisation.*

INTRODUCTION

India is a growing economy and consumer spending has been rising year on year. As per the report, *The New Indian: The Many Facets of a Changing Consumer*, published by BCG in March 2017, despite a conservative rise in GDP of mere 6%-7% a year, India's nominal year-over-year expenditure growth of 12% is more than double the anticipated global rate of 5% and will make India the third-largest consumer market by 2025. The report highlights that out of India's five household income categories (elite, affluent, aspirers, next billion and strugglers), the top two income classes are the fastest growing. From 2016 through 2025, the share of elite and affluent households will increase from 8% to 16% of the total while the share of strugglers will drop from 31% to 18%.

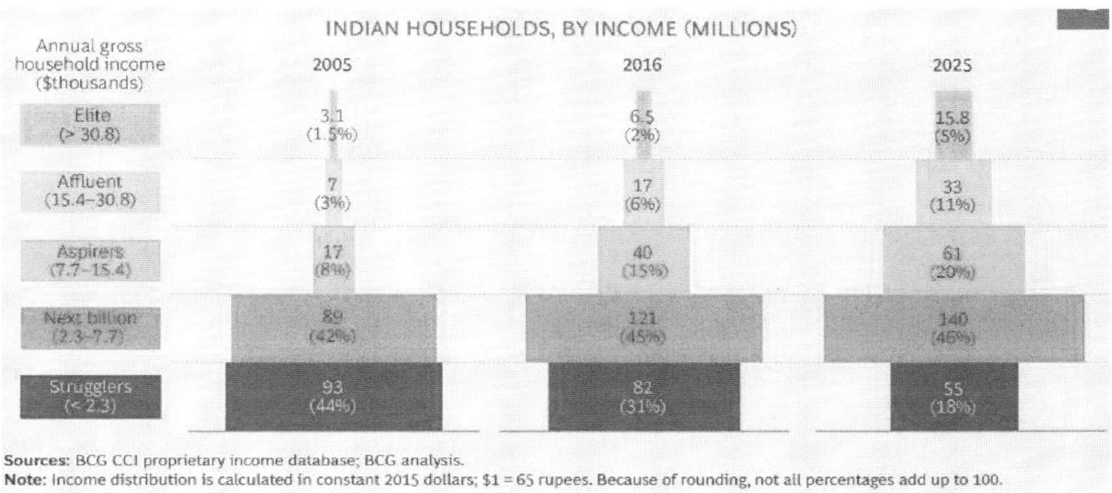

Figure 1: Income Distribution in Various Income Categories

The buying pattern in India has undergone a dramatic change in terms of both volume as well as the composition of purchase. The growing prosperity of people due to better job opportunities, aggressive digital exposure, rise in nuclear families and continuous urbanization has brought a rapid transformation in the demand pattern and demand cycle. This shift called for aggressive and innovative marketing strategies over the years and there are increasing number of products and brands being introduced in the market. The modern consumer is gripped with a constant urge to explore and adopt advanced products as a result of plethora of products and services made available to them due to incessant advertisements and promotional campaigns. In a marketing perspective, companies invest billions per year to study the customer behaviour and psychology. They conduct many surveys, interviews, observations to understand what the customer want and what he needs. This understanding drives them to know how to act to make the customer buying a product. With the research, companies are more proficient into controlling the market. In this way, marketing may propose some products that the customer did not imagine, did not ask for before. It proposes a product that was not expected by people and motivates the customer to buy it. This can be seen as controlling the customer in the company's advantage. Every stage of buying process is heavily influenced by the marketer. The advertising and marketing campaigns are intelligently and creatively created to push the customers towards increased purchase of products and usage of services. As compared to traditional marketing techniques when not many forms of marketing channels existed, the modern day marketing aggressively creates excess of demand, excess competition among producers, creates excess supply of products and overall creates an environment for conspicuous consumption. Many successful marketers regularly employ psychology in appealing to consumers. Smart, skillful, honest marketers use psychology legally, ethically, and respectfully to attract and engage consumers, and compel them to buy more. Marketing effect on consumer behaviour is a mix of influence as well as manipulation.

Figure 2: Buying process (adapted from Kotler et al., 2008)

India is now the sixth largest consumer economy, after the US, China, Japan, the UK and Germany. Consumption across the country is expected to almost triple over the next decade from the current $1.4 trillion to $4 trillion, according to the report titled *The New Indian: The Many Facets of a Changing Consumer*. The report is based on a survey of 10,000 consumers from 30 locations across the country conducted by BCG's Centre for Customer Insight. The rise in household consumption leads to rise in production and in turn leads to rise in generation of more and more unutilised, discarded and misused waste. According to a latest CPCB report, India produced 48 million tonnes of solid waste in 2008. By 2016, this figure had risen. India produced some 52 million tonnes of waste each year, or roughly 0.144 million tonnes per day, of which roughly

23 per cent is processed—taken to landfills or disposed using other technologies. Waste generation rate depends on factors such as population density, economic status, level of commercial activity, culture and city/region. India faces serious issues with waste management due to inadequate methods of waste collection, transportation, disposal and treatment. Current systems in India cannot cope with the volumes of waste generated by an increasing urban population and this impacts the environment and public health. The current waste management in India focuses on strategies and spreading awareness to cope up with the problem of waste management. Waste Management and handling rules to ensure proper waste management in India and new updated draft rules have been published. Municipal authorities are responsible for implementing these rules and developing infrastructure for collection, storage, segregation, transportation, processing and disposal of solid waste. The informal sector has a very important role in India and this must be integrated into formal SWM systems. The informal sector is characterized by small-scale, labour-intensive, largely unregulated and unregistered low-technology manufacturing or provision of materials and services. There has been a growing need in India to focus on issues of waste collection, transportation and treatment, engineered landfills, converting waste into energy, removal of barriers to improved waste management. Efforts are being taken both by government and social activists to spread awareness about waste treatment and Indians are realising their roles as individuals in contributing towards waste management, waste recycle and saving the natural resources. However, this paper attempts to address the issue of waste management at the point of origin and the role that a marketer can play in influencing the consumers in moulding the buying behaviour and adopt a reasonable and responsible pattern of household consumption. In reality, what we consume should be tied to where it is from and where it is going, not just because the stages are intrinsically connected, but because acknowledging a product's entire life cycle can strengthen our relationship with the product and make us want to consume it even more. Marketers can create campaigns, which focus on today's environmental problems and how they are linked to private consumption. They need to assume bigger responsibilities towards spreading awareness about consumption and its negative climate and environmental impact by releasing thought provoking ad campaigns and effective promotions. The government can create more programs, which promote sustainable consumption, and marketers can influence the affluent and urban segment to indulge more in buying recycled and upscaled products.

LITERATURE REVIEW

Effective marketing can encourage sustainable ways of consumption and influence consumers to contribute to environment by changing their behaviours. Consumers may experience obstacles in making a shift due to lack of information, unavailability of brands, which make sustainable goods, and inadequate outlets to purchase recycled and upscaled commodities. Indian urban audience needs to be addressed with a strategic and streamlined approach adopted by marketers. Marketing campaigns must focus on promoting the benefits of responsible purchase, benefits of producing durable products; promote services of fixing the damaged products rather than fast replacement of goods. Marketing campaigns can work on 5 point agenda; spread awareness for sustainable products among users, encourage demand for eco-friendly products, encourage producers to adopt ecological ways of manufacturing, encourage delay in discard and towards the end of the product life cycle, effective marketing can encourage systematic ways of disposal of unused commodities.

The clothing industry is the second largest polluter in the world, second only to oil. The overall impact that the apparel industry has on the planet is quite grim. Fashion is a complicated business involving long and varied supply chains of production, raw material, textile manufacture, clothing construction, shipping, retail and use and ultimately disposal of the garment. In the modern consumerist society, shopping has become a way of life, a weekly pastime and with the ease of online shopping for many it has become an addiction. Shopping malls, glossy fashion magazines, catalogues and internet ads lure consumers towards entertaining opportunities of spending money. Fast fashion feeds this unchecked consumerism and generates massive amount of cheap clothes, ultimately accelerating carbon emissions and global warming. A general assessment takes into account not only the obvious pollutants – the pesticides used in cotton farming, the toxic dyes used in manufacturing and the great amount of waste discarded clothing creates – but also the extravagant amount of natural resources used in extraction, farming, harvesting, processing, manufacturing and shipping. Fast fashion relies on globalised, mass production where garments are transformed from the design stage to the retail floor in only a few weeks. With retailers selling the latest fashion trends at very low prices, consumers are easily swayed to purchase more than they need. But this overconsumption comes with a hidden price tag, and it is the environment and workers in the supply chain that pay. Brands H&M, Tommy Hilfiger, Zara and the likes have been constantly criticized by social activists for promoting the fast fashion culture and adding to the fashion carbon footprint tremendously. Most global brands in past five-seven years have adopted measures to imbibe environment friendly manufacturing techniques like dry dyeing, clothes made from organic cotton, pollution emission control measures in textile and processing units. H&M and Zara, both purveyors of fast fashion, joined 33 other fashion companies in a pledge to increase their clothing recycling by 2020 and are collecting and recycling used clothing at many of their stores. Business growth is dependent on repeat purchases and in order to survive in the competitive era of global retailing, business houses direct the marketing departments to launch best possible ad campaigns which drive strong brand presence and brand loyalty.

As opposed to the fast fashion concept, there has been a revolutionary business strategy proposed by few brands like Patagonia, Cotopaxi, Cliffbar and company, Columbia bar, North Face and Osprey who have successfully implemented the culture of slow fashion. Slow Fashion represents all things "eco", "ethical" and "green" in one unified movement. It was first coined by Kate Fletcher, from the Centre for Sustainable Fashion, when fashion was compared to the Slow Food experience. The alarming rate of unaccounted consumption which leads to unaccounted heaps of garbage in landfills calls for effective communication to encourage and promote the slow fashion culture. The marketers need to drive strong values imparted by the slow fashion movement, which could never gain momentum vis a vis the fast fashion consumerist approach that grips the society at large.

Big fashion brands have started working around sustainability. Adidas created a trainer made entirely of yarns and filaments reclaimed and recycled from ocean waste and illegal deep-sea gillnets. Nike made socks, shorts and jerseys from shredded, recycled plastic bottles for the United States' 2015 Women's World Cup uniforms and since 2010 the company has diverted more than two billion plastic bottles from landfills into recycled polyester. Nike is one of the pioneer brand that works towards sustainable innovation and works under three verticals: minimize environmental footprint, transform manufacturing, and unleash human potential.

Patagonia, the outdoor clothing brand, is known for various environmental sustainability efforts. The privately held company has been known to promote used wear and the brand stands out due to the deep social and environmental connect that the brand propagates. Patagonia team claims to be rebels from the consumer culture. Patagonia has leveraged its position as a top outdoor gear and clothing brand to advocate for environmental causes. In spite of what looks like an anti-marketing effort, the company has actually seen its revenues grow in the last few years--despite the recession. Yvon Chouinard, founder Patagonia has pushed Patagonia to adopt sustainable practices, including making fabric out of recycled plastic bottles. The marketing strategies adopted by team Patagonia supports the mission and vision of the company. The most debatable advertisement of printed full-page ad in *The New York Times*, On Black Friday 2011, that encouraged customers to not buy its products resonated with the sentiments of the socially driven consumer segment. The activist company offers free repairs for its apparel, to promote the slow fashion culture. Patagonia's environmental efforts are genuine and it has the track record to prove its authenticity. In the early 1990s, Patagonia started using organic cotton, and its buyers coached Nike and the Gap on how to make the switch. At the beginning of the millennium, Patagonia partnered with fly fishing equipment outfit Blue Ribbon Flies to create 1% for the Planet, a coalition of businesses that pledged to donate 1% of their sales to grassroots environmental groups. In 2009, Patagonia collaborated with Wal-mart to spread awareness about how the retail giant could adopt more sustainable practices. The success of Patagonia lies in the fact that the companies philosophy was made to resonate with the identified target audience. As the company has tapped into more consumers in the environment friendly target market, they have managed to expand their sales. As a result of successful marketing, Patagonia has opened 40 stores globally since 2011. Even as Patagonia has led an effort to expand the useful life of its products, an effort that is at odds with the planned obsolescence approach of many manufacturers today, it has seen its sales rise. The advertisements released to match the sentiments of the target audience helped the company's environmentally friendly efforts. More of these people are buying Patagonia products as they see the company's long-lasting wares as a way to express their values.

As mentioned earlier, consumer behavior is influenced by many things, including environmental and marketing factors, the situation, personal and psychological factors, family and culture. Businesses try to figure out trends so they can reach the people most likely to buy their products in the most cost-effective way possible. Businesses often try to influence a consumer's behavior with things they can control such as the layout of a store, music, grouping and availability of products, pricing, and most strategically through advertising and promotional campaigns. Indian urban (esp rich and affluent) consumer segment which is considered to be most responsible for wasteful consumption needs to be made aware of responsible purchasing through the five point agenda discussed earlier. Marketers in India need to assume bigger roles in encouraging conscious buying and promoting environment friendly Indian brands like bhu:sattva, Forty red bangles, No nasties and Upasana. These brands are working with the possibilities for reusing leftover and discarded fabrics. Doodlage, is one such brand whose creative director Kriti Tula uses dead stock and industrial waste with organic cotton and sustainable materials. In their AW16 collection, titled Hopscotch, the design team used corn and banana fabric to substitute cotton and yarn made entirely from spinning rejects. The increasing emphasis on minimal waste leads almost naturally to the concept of recycling and upcycling. (Contrary to what one might think, the two are not the same. Recycling refers to reuse, while upcycling is the process of turning discarded items into a product of great value). Jewellery designer Advaeita Mathur who runs Studio Metallurgy has converted plumbing washers into jewellery while Amit Agarwal has constructed garments from discarded bindi sheets. Lakme Fashion Week (2017), one of the country's most successful industry events, dedicated an entire day to upcycling and sustainability. The Artisans' Centre "Reincarnations Show" turned the spotlight on new and emerging brands—Jambudweep was a spectacle of products crafted from non-hazardous industrial waste while the Wandering Whites label showcased jewellery made from a mix of stones, brass, industrial waste and scrap. The brand I Was a Sari also showcased a variety of designs all made from recycled saris.

While the Indian fashion fraternity has initiated the launch of sustainable products and initiated the use of discard for producing recycled and upscaled goods across lifestyle categories, the Indian marketers need to provide the much required platform to these designers and product developers. International brands like Patagonia and Cotopaxi can be taken as inspirational fashion brands in this context. The marketing campaigns were successful despite releasing unconventional advertisements which encouraged reduced consumption. Advertisements with bold taglines "Less is more" and "Do not buy this jacket" (as it lasts long) and releasing social campaigns urging consumers to mend their clothes, shoes, accessories and other household products rather than throwing them away were well received by the international consumers. The marketing campaigns, which were meant to educate consumers towards cautious buying, were initially marked by a business philosophy which was detrimental to business growth. However, the strong emotional connect between the brands and the target audience led to instantaneous success of the clothing line. Based on his ownership of Patagonia, FORBES pegs Yvon Chouinard's net worth at $1 billion dated March 2017.

RESEARCH METHODOLOGY

The research involved a survey to assess the impact that marketing and promotional campaigns can create in influencing the urban fashion conscious consumer in favour of less spending and sustainable purchasing pattern. The objective of the survey was to assess if consumers from the rich and affluent class respond to marketing campaigns which encourage less spending and exhibit signs of responsible purchase decisions for fashion and lifestyle products. The sample segment: the questionnaire was sent to 50 consumers of fashion products (backed by strong purchasing power) comprising of designers, students from premium fashion schools, teachers, working professionals from IT industry and homemakers. 35 responses were received. Respondents' age ranged from 23-45 years. The survey questions were designed to understand whether the fashion conscious consumers feel social conscious towards the issue of waste management. The interview and focused group discussion was framed as one on one conversation with fifteen individuals, identified as fashion forward clients who represent the fast fashion shopper group in India. The feedbacks from respondents highlighted that 51% of the sample audience are aware and willing to know more, while 29% of respondents believe strongly in the concept of responsible consumption. 60% of respondent are aware of brands who work on recycled clothing and 55% of respondent shared strong urge to connect with brands or organisations which support less spending and sustainable clothing. The research also reconfirmed the popularity of social media as the most influential emerging marketing channel. 82% of the respondents shared support in favour of the statement "Effective marketing both (online and offline) can create social awareness for reduced purchase pattern, purchase of recycled and upscaled products and support responsible consumer behaviour in favour of waste management". *Refer to annexure for survey questions and responses*. The interview session with chosen target audience who indulge in constant shopping and patronise fast fashion brought clarity that if more awareness is spread, the urban consumer is willing to adopt the ecological shopping concept, willing to patronise the nature loving brands and also willing to associate with recycled old clothes promoted for social cause.

SUMMARY

Slow Fashion encourages a systems thinking approach. Strong marketing campaigns especially social media campaigns in favour of need based buying, reusing and fixing old and used garments, footwear, handbags and accessories can impact collective choices of consumer groups and affect the environment and people. Business houses in India need to restructure their business models such that they focus on manufacturing models that support sustainable innovation. The marketers need to bring about a change in the way the brand and products are pushed in the market and help consumers develop conscious buying habits. Designers can meet human needs by co-creating garments and marketers can shape consumer culture by offering fashion with emotional significance. Encouraging classic design over passing trends will contribute to the longevity of garments. A number of Slow Fashion designers are ensuring the longevity of their clothing by sourcing high quality fabrics, offering traditional cuts and creating beautiful, timeless pieces. Overall, the buying habits need to be moulded for both offline and online purchases, fashion and non-fashion segments. Responsible demands relieve pressure on natural cycles so production can be in a healthy rhythm with what the earth can provide. Creative marketing techniques which examine the consumer decision-making model and strategically arouse social sentiments can contribute in shaping an environmental friendly shopping environment. Brands backed by well-established business houses along with government support can align promotional campaigns to arouse awareness towards saving natural resources. Promoting eco-friendly brands combined with social messages can not only benefit the businesses by winning emerging segment of socially aware customers but also aid in tiding over strong competition that Indian brands face vis a vis the international brands. Apparel leads second in waste generation all over world and the problem looks grim in an over populated country like India. The Indian audience needs more awareness about eco-friendly, recycled and upscaled products and overall awareness about how to restrain the household purchase to support responsible consumer behaviour. The business economics of fashion houses need to be reworked and strategically target the chosen audience who are ready but unable to adopt the new culture of "saving while during purchasing". Awareness drive led by the urban consumer and led for the urban consumer can cure the problem of waste generation at the point of consumption which in reality is the point of origin of waste. There is immense scope for marketers to mould the consumer behaviour in favour of industry and society at large.

REFERENCES

[1] Kearney, A.T. (2016), Retail in the Era of the Connected Customer: Perspectives on How Indian Retailers can Win in Today's World of Connected Customers, Retailers Association of India, Available: http://rls.net.in/wp-content/uploads/2016/11/AT_Kearney_RLS_Summit_Whitepaper_Final.pdf

[2] Gugnani, A. and Brahma, K.P. (2015), Fashion Retail Scenario in India: Trends and Market Dynamics, http://www.technopak.com/Files/fashion-retail-scenario-in-india.pdf

[3] Kumar, S., Smith, S. R., Fowler, G., Velis, C., Kumar, S.J., Arya, S., Kumar, R. and Cheeseman, C. (2017), Challenges and Opportunities Associated with Waste Management in India, *Royal Society Open Science*, 4 (3), pp. 1-21.

[4] Evans, M., Jamal, A. and Foxall, G. (2009), Consumer Behaviour, 2nd edition, John Wiley and Sons Ltd., Publication.

[5] Levy, M., Weitz, B. and Pandit, A. (2012), Retailing Management, 8th edition, McGraw Hill Education (India) Private Limited Publication.

[6] Sinha, P.K. and Uniyal, D.P. (2012), Managing Retailing, 2nd edition, Oxford Publication.

[7] https://www.bcg.com/en-in/publications/2017/marketing-sales-globalization-new-indian-changing-consumer.aspx

[8] http://www.government.se/articles/2016/10/strategy-for-sustainable-consumption/

[9] https://www.pymnts.com/in-depth/2015/retail-growth-by-not-growing/

ANNEXURE – I

Questionnaire

Social awareness towards responsible buying behaviour

This survey is an attempt to understand role of advertising and promotional campaigns in spreading awareness for sustainable and slow fashion.

Question No. 5

What influences your urge to buy more fashion and lifestyle products? Choose the most influential factor.

- ☐ Informative advertisements and promotional offers
- ☐ Fashion and lifestyle trends observed online and offline
- ☐ Celebrity lifestyles and trends that social icons set
- ☐ Peer group

Response

What influences your urge to buy more fashion and lifestyle products? Choose the most influential factor.

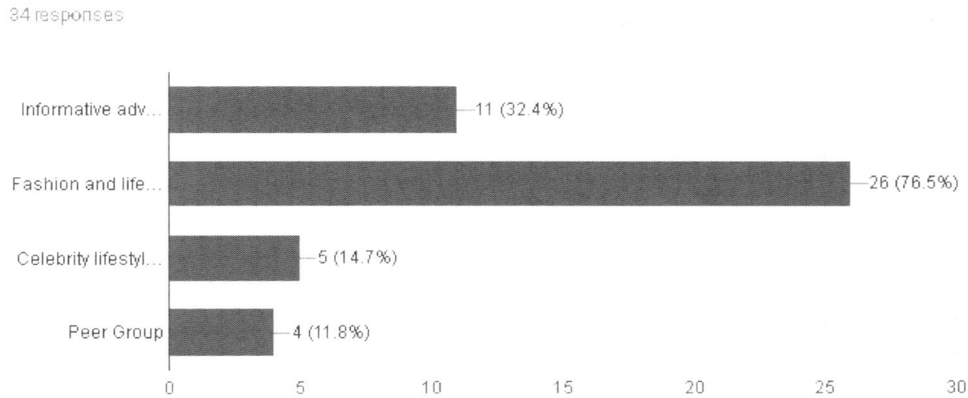

Question No. 6

Which form of advertisement influences you the most? Choose the most preferred option from below:

- ☐ TV ads
- ☐ Print ad in fashion and lifestyle magazines
- ☐ Social media campaigns
- ☐ Celebrity endorsements
- ☐ Billboards and hoardings

Response

Which form of advertisement influences you the most? Choose the most preferred option from below:

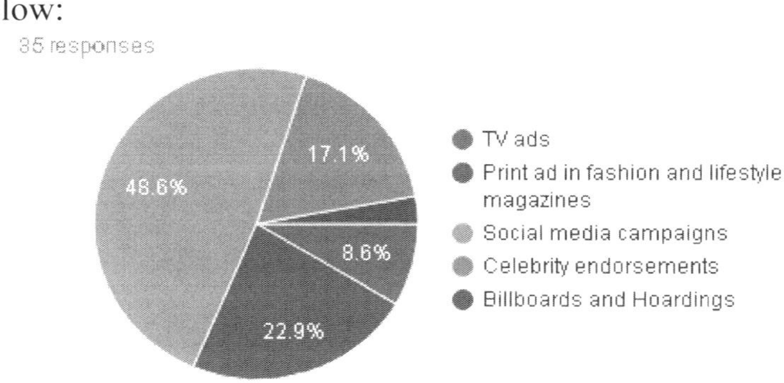

Question No. 9

Share your response to the tagline – "Less now is more later". Reduce, Reuse and Save for planet.

☐ Strongly agree and need more reinforcement of this concept

☐ Understand somewhat but need clarity

☐ Understand as I have read about this concept

Response

Share your response to the tagline – "Less now is more later". Reduce, Reuse and Save for planet.

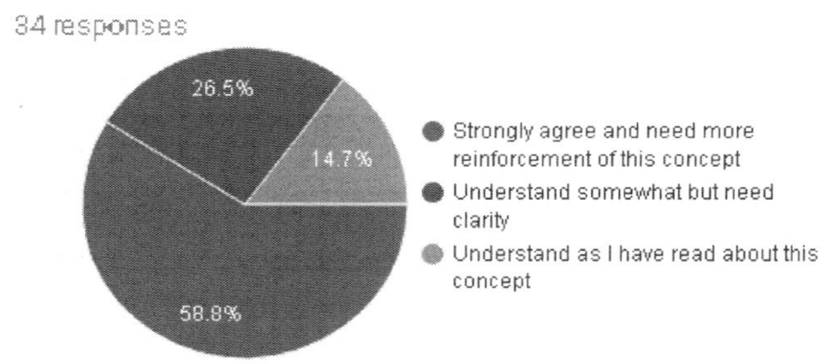

Question No. 10

Share your response to the tagline – "Buy products that last long and not fast gone".

☐ Strongly agree and need more reinforcement of this concept

☐ Understand and search for such products

☐ Understand somewhat but need clarity

☐ Disagree with concept as it affects my lifestyle

Response

Share your response to the tagline – "Buy products that last long and not fast gone".

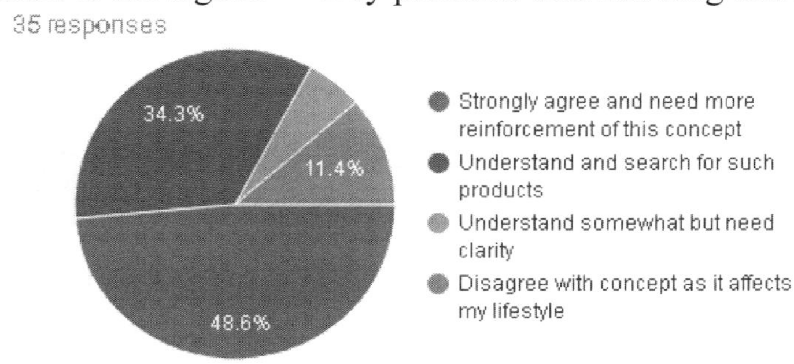

Question No. 11

Share your response to the tagline – "Be responsible and not just fashionable. I support Slow Fashion!"

☐ I feel connected with this thought

☐ I need better understanding

☐ I do not understand this concept as I have not heard or read about it

☐ Yes I have heard of this concept and feel responsible to promote it further

Response

Share your response to the tagline – "Be responsible and not just fashionable. I support Slow Fashion!"

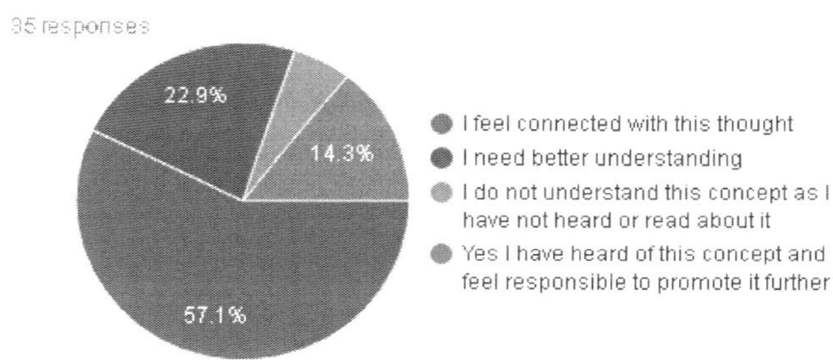

ANNEXURE – II

Questionnaire – Focused Group Discussion and Interview Session

Social awareness towards responsible buying behaviour

This survey is an attempt to understand role of advertising and promotional campaigns in spreading awareness for sustainable and slow fashion.

1. Do you believe that modern society is marked by a consumerist approach?
2. What can the socially aware citizen do to drive the "less is more" concept? Are you willing to join any such promotional campaign which is intended to work towards making the modern consumer aware about reduced spending and switch to eco-friendly products which last longer and leads to less wastage?
3. Marketers play an important role in driving more purchases? Please share your views on what kinds of advertisements and promotional campaigns attract you the most. Social media ads are most influential. Have you seen enough social media ads on waste management, responsible purchasing, and recycled clothing? Please share your views with regards to this scenario.

4. Which brands do you follow and why? (Apparel and lifestyle) What brands drive encouragement to you as a consumer?
5. You have shared feedback through questionnaire survey that you hold interest in concept of recycled and upsclaed clothing or brands which patronise similar concepts. Please share you view on few Indian brands that are working on these lines.
6. Share your feedback for below images: Don't you feel such strong advertisements work against the urban lifestyle concept? If not, what makes you interested and why would you still associate yourself with such brands?

Image 1

Image 2

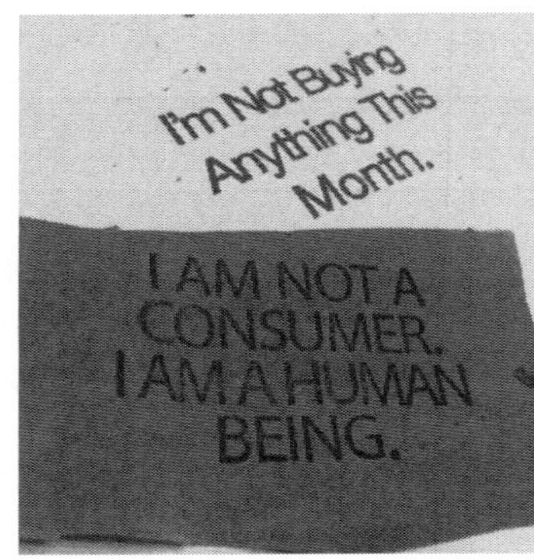

Image 3

Image 4

Value Addition of Waste *Reed mace* and *Rice straw* Used for Wagoo Weaving through Colour

PROMIL PANDE[1], ANJALI AGRAWAL[2] AND SAGAR SINGH[2]

[1] *Ansal University, Sushant School of Art and Architecture, Golf Course Road, Gurugram, India*

[2] *G D Goenka University, Sohna Road, Gurugram, India*

E-mail: promilpande@gmail.com; anjali.agrawal@gdgoenka.ac.in

ABSTRACT

Wagoo weaving in Kashmir is an indigenous artisanal activity practiced since the 16th century. A grass mat made from reed mace and agricultural residues such as rice straw both grow in abundance so are sourced locally making it a sustainable, eco-friendly, biodegradable commodity produced by home-based workers. Women enabling them to augment and support their family income predominantly practice the craft. The natural gold hues of the grass and its insulation properties make it suitable for use in any season. Traditionally a popular choice amongst Kashmiris for thatched shelters and floor mats, it played a vital role in the social and economic prosperity of the community. In this paper, natural beautiful yellows and red colour was introduced in wagoo weaving to enable these mats to compete and coexist with the mass-produced colorful acrylic blankets and Ethylene Vinyl Acetate foam sheets that have started replacing the original wagoo.

Keywords: *Craft, Natural dyes, Residue, Sustainability.*

INTRODUCTION

Peanch is the Kashmiri vernacular term for the raw material used in wagoo weaving. *Typha Elephantina* and *Typha Angustata*, which grows abundantly in and around Mir Behri Dal and Anchar lake, District Srinagar; Shadipora and adjoining areas, district Bandipora and Talpora village, district Budgam. This marshy plant grows to a height of 2.5 meters, the smooth deep green leaves that turn a golden yellow when dry are about 120 to 180cms long and 1.8 to 3.8 cms broad. The leaves used for mat weaving are manually harvested in the months from August-September and dried in open fields in the form of erect bundles.

As home-based workers (Pearson, 2004), it is primarily the women who engage in wagoo weaving in addition to their household chores. Portable looms are set up in the

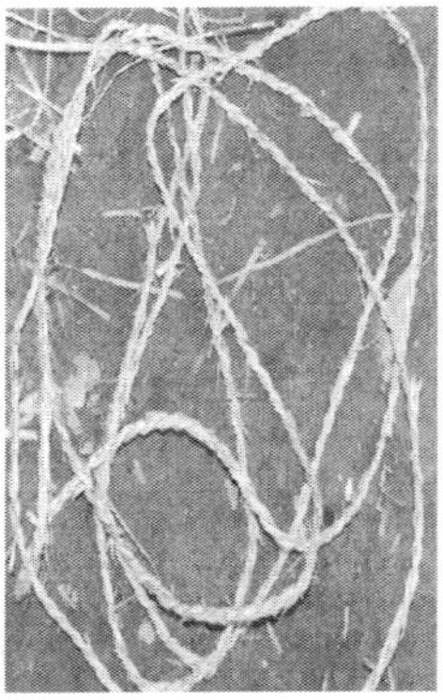

(a) Rice Straw (b) Peanch (c) Patij

Figure 1: Grass Used for Wagoo Weaving

open courtyard outside the house to enable the process. The warp for the wagoo mat is made out of patij while peanch is used for the weft. A product created from agricultural residue, patij is an S twisted grass rope (Image 1c) made by manually twisting a few strands of pre-soaked rice straw at a time. The S twisted rope, approximately 1 cm thick is stretched across two beams of the loom, front beam (cloth beam) and the rear beam (warp beam). Numbers of warps are determined by the width of the mat to be woven, and warps are spaced 6-8 cms apart. The weave structure of the wagoo is predominantly a plain /tabby weave or its variation the basket weave (Pande, 2016). Traditionally both the patij and the peanch are used in its natural form and color, giving the wagoo a beautiful natural golden hue making the wagoo a sustainable, biodegradable mat. The rhythmical interlacing of the grass resulting in a useful aid used ubiquitously by Kashmiris in homes and boats especially as floor coverings (Jaitley, 1990). With a lifespan of two years, the wagoo mat an outcome of the age-

Figure 2: Wagoo Weaving in Progress

old, handed down culture of wagoo weaving, traditionally, was an artisanal activity connecting and combining within the social fabric the craft persons the producer, and the consumer (Chattopadhyay, 1985). The wagoo artisans as in the case of other Indian crafts communities are close-knit, traditional communities bound by kinship, caste, and occupational ties. (Venkatesan, 2006)

In recent years however the *wagoo* has seen a decline in demand, one of the reasons cited by the weavers interviewed was the influx of cheaper colorful mass produced imported acrylic blankets and Ethylene Vinyl Acetate foam sheets. The once popular *wagoo* mats, which was a thriving industry contributing to the social, cultural and economic well being and prosperity of the community was no longer a dependable home-based activity. The younger family members no longer seeing a future in pursuing the craft of *wagoo* weaving are looking for alternative employment sources to augment the family income. This would not pose a serious problem but for the fact that if the *peanch* is left unharvested, the lakes where the grass grows will turn into marshlands and subsequently to land patches eventually leading to choking of the lakes. Thus the wagoo mats are not only a means of employment and financial security to the local industry that engaged almost every household in the community (Yassir, 2016) but is an essential link in creating and retaining a sustainable ecological system in Kashmir. However, over time there has been a steady decline in the demand for the *wagoo*-mat because of the broader range of industrialized designs, styles, and materials available in the floor-covering category at competitive prices. Adding value through dying the grass, which can be subsequently used to weave colorful patterns to add variety and diversity, is an attempt at revitalizing the craft by enabling a ‘closer fit between human intentions and the ecological systems’ (Orr, 2002, p. 11).

DYEING

(a) **Pre-mordanting of grass:** The peanch and patij grass samples were premordanted with 10% owf alum, ferrous sulphate and copper sulphate at 80°C for 30 minutes. The samples were then dried.

(b) **Dyeing with natural dyes:** The pre-mordanted grass was then dyed with 5% owf turmeric and alizarin at 80°C for 1 hour to assess the feasibility of dyeing. The material to liquor ratio was maintained at 1:40. The dyed grass samples were then cold rinsed and hot rinsed.

(c) **Weaving of the dyed samples:** The grass samples were found to give beautiful yellow to brown colour with turmeric and shades of red with alizarin as shown in Figure 3.

The samples were plain woven using the dyed grass. Cotton yarn was taken as warp and dyed grass was taken as weft.

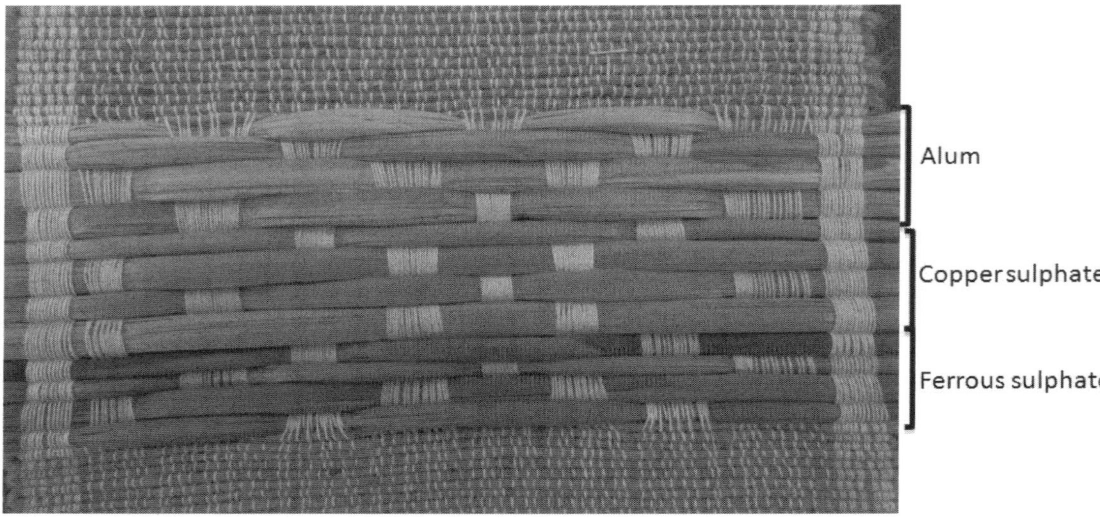

(a)

(b)

Figure 3: Dyed Grass Woven as Wagoo Mat

Thus, through the preliminary study it can be seen that the dyed grass samples have enhanced the appearance of the wagoo mat and hence, it will increase the value of the wagoo mat made from waste grass samples.

CONCLUSION

Wagoo mat is made from reed mace and agricultural residues such as rice straw in Kashmir. The grass, otherwise a waste, grows in abundance and is sourced locally making it a sustainable, eco-friendly, biodegradable commodity. The waste grass was dyed with natural dyes such as turmeric and alizarin and woven in plain weave, hence adding value to the product.

REFERENCES

[1] Adamson, G. (2016), *Thinking through Craft*. Bloomsbury.

[2] Chattopadhyay, K. (1985), *Handicrafts of India*. Indian Council for Cultural Relations. New Delhi.

[3] Jaitly, J. (1990), *Crafts of Jammu, Kashmir and Ladakh* (pp. 36-57). Mapin Publishing Pvt. Ltd., Ahmedabad.

[4] Orr, David W. (2002), *The Nature of Design: Ecology, Culture and Human Intention*. Oxford University press.

[5] Pearson, R. (2004), Organizing Home-based Workers in the Global Economy: An Action Based Research Approach, *Development in Practice*, 14 (1-2).

[6] Pande, P. et al. (2016), The Languishing Craft of Wagoo Weaving: Design Interventions and the Revitalization of Indigenous Craft Tradition, *International Conference Proceedings: 3D Printing and Rapid Manufacturing and Sustainability in Design*, Bloomsbury, New Delhi.

[7] Rana, E.C. (2008), Sustainable Local Development through One Town One Product (OTOP): The Case of OTOP Movement in Mindanao, Philippines. *Journal of OVOP Policy*, 1, 31-38.

[8] Sennett, R. (2008), *The Craftsman*, London: Allen Lane.

[9] Venkatesan, S. (2005), Shifting Balances in a 'Craft Community': The Mat Weavers of Pattamadai, South India, *Contributions to Indian Sociology*.

[10] Yassir, A. (2016), *Wagoo: Traditional Kashmir Mat Falling Flat in Face of Polymer Onslaught*, Greater Kashmir.

The Environmentally-Friendly Chains for the Fashion-Driven Design Industry

For a Fashion Industry 4.0

ROBERTO LIBERTI

Università degli Studi della Campania Luigi Vanvitelli, Dipartimento DADI, Italy
E-mail: roberto.liberti@unicampania.it

ABSTRACT

What we want to propose in this paper are the researches carried out by the FA.RE. (1) Fashion Research Lab of the University of Campania Luigi Vanvitelli is doing a decade on an ideal model of Zero Emission industrial district in the Italian textile clothing sector. Starting from an analysis of the area of the existing compartments in the various manufacturing sectors of the fashion system, a system of 'advanced sustainable interaction' is being analyzed among different companies but able to cooperate mutually among themselves in the 'zero emission' optics. Different case studies will show this advanced search program that in some cases is already applied and working.

Keywords: *Sustainable, Industrial district, Zero emission, Component, Enironmental requirements for industrial products, Eco design, Life cycle.*

INTRODUCTION

Textile-Clothing is a sector of great economic importance for Italy. This is the third national manufacturing sector, which nowadays has almost 450,000 employees and more than 50,000 companies active in the territory, accounting for about 10% of the Value added of the Italian Manifacturer. Despite its top-orchestral role, or perhaps precisely because of this, the textile industry is under close attention to the sustainability of the various phases that make up its chain. Textile productions are often characterized by processes that are significantly impacting the environment, especially in terms of consumption of natural resources (first water), electricity consumption and use of chemicals; particularly in wet processes such as dyeing, printing and finishing, the high consumption of water and chemicals is charged.

TA represents the sixth most productive activity that emits on greenhouse gas emissions – about 10% of global emissions for 3.4 million tonnes in 2011 - with consumption of:

- 1,074 million kWh of electricity,
- 132 million tons of coal,
- 6-9 billion liters of water.

Since it has entered the common vocabulary, the concept of "Sustainability" has assumed various meanings and extensions, from time to time applied to reference contexts. In recent years, attention has been paid to environmental sustainability issues that have led the textile industry to be subjected to heavy criticisms of environmental impacts and human health from residues of substances on products and production processes associated with it. The issue of ecology is triggered by issues related to environmental emergency, waste of natural resources, energy costs, global warming, global overpopulation and the resulting depletion of habitats, shortage of raw materials, toxicity some industrial products, air and water pollution, waste disposal. Being ecologically sustainable, today means making choices that can lower the environmental impact of their productive activities, contain consumption, design and build objects for the raw materials used, the ways in which they have been used worked, end-of-life behavior, diminish the impact on the environment.

ENVIRONMENTAL BALANCE FOR INDUSTRIAL DISTRICT

We have long been aware of the situation of degradation that has occurred due to a planning of the development of production activities that takes into minimum consideration the problems and impacts on the environment. This awareness by the civil society has led to the definition of multiple actions for the environmental protection compared to past years. Many changes have also been made thanks to the sensitivity procured by ecological policies that, in addition to compliance with stricter environmental control standards, have set up a decentralized decision-making process, optimal for the accountability of the actors involved for the dynamics related to the sustainability of production processes on the environment . In this scenario, many tools have been disseminated, useful for planning and managing the environmental impacts of production processes, such as the 'environmental balance'. This budget is able to include the environmental aspects within the management of the planning of the activities themselves. A useful tool, therefore, to identify those critical points of impact that production activities have on the environment, in terms of resource consumption and waste production, in order to

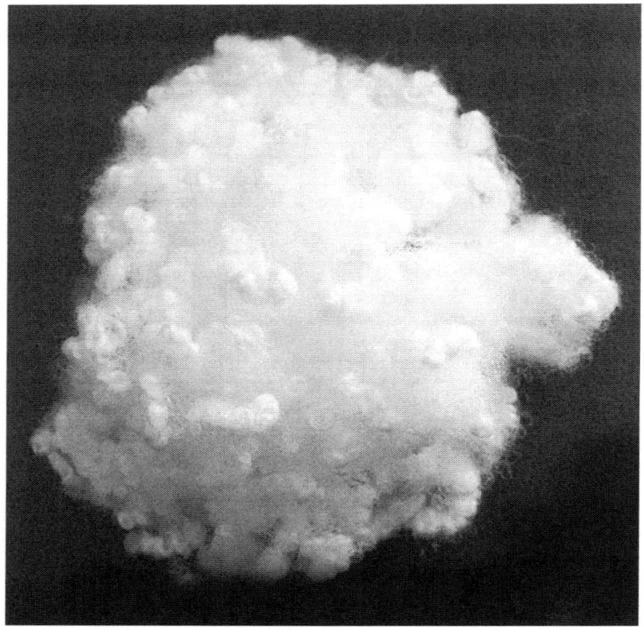

Figure 1: Bottle Fiber in Recycled Polyester Pet Staple

make those improvements to the process itself in terms of eco-orientation. In terms of impact on the environment, the environmental balance can be defined as a very useful tool for the quantization of releases produced in the environment in terms of waste in air, water, etc., to arrive at the assessment of a level of environmental efficiency related to the various activities to improve the status of the territories in which the companies are incorporated.

This system can make an important contribution to the identification of the fields of improvement on which it is essential to act to reduce the environmental impacts of industrial activities within a given industrial district. The district represents one of the forms of industrial aggregation on which an analysis has been carried out in this last decade in Italy and which can represent an interesting model of study for other similar territorial cases, even extranational. The environmental balance for a given industrial district allows, in fact, to provide the district in question with a considerable information base, through which it is possible to activate processes of 'environmental communication'. This is possible thanks to the environmental reports and the statements that the various entrepreneurs are called to conduct in which it is also necessary to define the environmental policies undertaken to make improvements in terms of reducing the impact on the environment.

A clear and transparent communication of environmental issues allows, in fact, to further raise awareness on issues related to environmental sustainability issues, deepening its environmental commitment and the results achieved in terms of improving the quality of life, creating relationships of trust with the community to which these benefits are addressed. The realization of an environmental balance for an industrial district must include an integrated analysis through environmental management systems and methodologies known internationally (ISO 14001, EMAS) thanks to a collaboration of both companies and public bodies that manage the territory. In this regard it is interesting to analyze the variables developed in the so-called "state-pressure-response" model by the Canadian statistician Antony Friend, a model later adopted by the Organization for Economic Cooperation and Development (OECD). This model organizes the indicators necessary to describe the environmental problems of a given geographical area in three different categories (status, pressure and response) interacting with each other according to cause and effect relationships. According to these reports, human works generate interactions on the environment (pressures) that impact on the various environmental subsystems (state). It is then the community to intervene with appropriate responses on the environment with suitable initiatives (responses), reducing the analyzed pressures of human activities, for example, with rehabilitation actions.

This model is widely used for its ability to interact with the various components involved in analyzing problems through:

- Identification of the environmental problem;
- Analysis and management of improvement;
- Continuous monitoring and evaluation of the environmental policy to be adopted.

With regard to the analysis of an environmental balance for a complex production site or an industrial district, the elements of "pressure" produced by the site are constituted by the input flows (consumption of water, electricity, fuels, etc.) and output (release of polluting emissions into water, soil and atmosphere). In this discussion, therefore, are the territorial variables in the analysis of a given site to allow the identification of adequate indicators able to describe the environmental status of the site and the implemented responses.

The results of this environmental analysis process, together with the information used for the analysis are codified through data and indicators that provide the basic elements for the communication phase facing outwards. These collected data are finally finalized to the diffusion of the same to the users and therefore to the community that represents the last and most important link. This analysis can be useful for the planning of environmental defense interventions of the territory and, in the specific case, will allow to show how industrial districts and poles operating in the fashion sector turn out to be productive sectors that can be governed also in terms of environmental impact.

With this in mind, many companies are starting to change their organizational structure to deal with environmental problems in advance by adopting 'green marketing' strategies and investing significant resources for environmental protection. This process should be part of a wider and more global project for an action that is actually aimed at closing the cycles of product existence: on the model of natural cycles, all the production and consumption processes triggered by human activities should also follow a circular course.

TECHNOLOGIES OF REGENERATION OF TEXTILE MATERIALS AND NEW PRODUCTS FOR INTERIOR DESIGN

Starting from the analysis of one of the industrial districts of the Campania textile and clothing industry and precisely that of San Marco dei Cavoti, an analysis was carried out for the environmental balance which led to analyzing a material considered as material during the verification of the outputs produced by the district. first for a 'second life' product. This research path was conducted with the FA.RE laboratory. of Campano University and some companies of the textile district, contacted thanks to the Chamber of Commerce of Benevento. The analysis carried out made it possible to analyze the district and the production fundamentally of packaging of jackets and coats. This district was born as a fasonist following the growth in the 90s of the Italian brand POP84, then saw the growth of companies in the district for many other brands such as the second lines of Dolce and Gabbana, Cavalli, Versace, Trussardi, etc.

In the processing of the winter collections of jackets and coats produced by about 50 companies (in the golden period of the district) the production of a high quantity of the waste of a special quality polyester fiber for upholstery, of fineness of 3,4 and exempt, was verified from waste and regenerated of polyester fiber or any other synthetic fiber. In the search for a possible recycling of this by-product of the textile industry, we analyzed studies conducted in collaboration with researchers and experts in materials chemistry, provided by the company CIEMME (2) of Molinara – Benevento – who have demonstrated the possibility of using this polyester wadding for a great variety of subsequent uses. This study starts from the analyzes carried out with ASSORIMAP (Italian Association of Plastics Recycling) that show the possibility of reprocessing the polyester according to two production methods: full conversion of the polyester and the complete conversion of the polyester.

Reconversion of the Polyester

This conversion has similar processing prerogatives to those adopted for the physical recycling of PET which also belongs to the family of polyesters. In fact, the physical recycling of this material allows the reuse of the polymer through its fusion and transformation into different products. The polyester waste can in fact be subjected to extrusion to be then transformed into sheets and sheets to be thermoformed; they can thus be used for the production of hollow containers for non-food uses. In addition to packaging, recycled polyester is widely used in the textile sector: in fact, by melting and spinning the polyester polymer, fibers, staples and filaments are obtained.

In this sense these are the most common uses for recycled polyester:

- staple for winter clothing padding;

Figure 2: Curtains Carpet Made with Polyester Spillage of the District as Internal Insulation and Silk Waste from the San Leucio Silk District for the Exterior

- staple for padding of mattresses;
- filtering felt of kitchen hoods
- thermal insulation felt for building;
- material for padding of motorcycle helmets;
- Non-woven fabric for environmental engineering works.

This recycling system has, in truth, a flaw identified by American researchers William McDonough and his colleague chemist Michael Braungart, who have shown that such a procedure produces a small amount of antimony, toxic heavy metal. This demonstrates how research in the field of environmental sustainability must never stop to solve problems upstream or downstream of current production processes, which need to constantly check the short and long-term causes on human health.

Partial Processing of Materials for an Industrial District 'Zero Emission'

A second hypothesis concerns the use of polyester waste sent to a second separate collection and to a subsequent shredding or granulation and then led to a partial processing that allows the reconstitution of a continuous polyester mat – without carrying out a physical recycling – which can then be used by coupling its characteristics with those of other thermoplastic materials such as PET or PE. Some hypotheses of use of this polyester mattress for long life products are:

- creation of products for outdoor garden furniture such as benches, benches, tables, etc.;
- naval industry for the realization of the naval diportistica;
- furniture industry.

What is of particular interest to us is the possibility of interacting the life cycle of waste polyester with that of other thermoplastic materials for which we can think of a recovery and a subsequent recycling. In this sense, observers have been activated on the reality of the disposal of plastic materials for the Campania region, useful to include this local initiative in a wider panorama to the regional territory. This second method of recovery of polyester waste in the analyzed textile district has the advantage of not requiring expensive investments for the management of new industrial plants such as those necessary for the conversion of PET into new polyester fiber to be filed, with processes that do not generate hazardous substances chemicals harmful to human health. Design experiments have been carried out with companies in the district in question to create, for example, thermo-acoustically insulating curtains/rugs for interiors, made with polyester spillage of the district as internal insulation and silk waste from the San Leucio silk district for the exterior of the curtains/carpet.

CONCLUSION

This demonstrates another value of the "Zero Emission" industry concept represented by the mutually collaborated collaboration of different companies and not necessarily in the same territory. In this perspective, strategic design can provide methods for the environmentally conscious management of industrial processes, up to the management of the design product. Such process/product innovation in the environmentally conscious fashion oriented sector is the ideal answer to the global problem of the emission of industrial waste in the environment, starting from research applied to companies in the fashion system object of this paper.

REFERENCES

[1] Basse, E.M. (2013), *Environmental Law in Denmark,* Kluwer Law International.

[2] Borzi, A. (2014), Il riparto di potestà legislative in materia di tutela dell'ambiente e dell'ecosistema alla luce della legislazione vigente in materia di rifiuti: gli spazi per la potestà attuativo-integrativa delle Regioni, in www.federalismi.it, n. 7 Borzi A., La gestione dei rifiuti, in Trattato di diritto dell'Ambiente, a cura di Sandulli M.A. e Ferrara, R., Milano, Giuffrè ed.

[3] Bucello, M., Piscitelli, L. & Viola, S.E. (2012), *VAS, VIA, AIA, rifiuti, emissioni in atmosfera*, Milano, Giuffrè ed.

[4] Caravita Di Toritto B. (2005), *Diritto dell'ambiente*, Il Mulino, Bologna, III ed.

[5] De Leonardis, F. (2011), *I rifiuti: dallo smaltimento alla prevenzione*, in Diritto dell'Ambiente – II edizione, Torino, G. Giappichelli Editore, pp. 303-317.

[6] De Sadeleer, N. (2005), New Perspectives on the Definition of Waste in EC, in *Journal of European Environmental & Planning Law*, Vol. 1, No. 4, pp. 46-58.

[7] Dell'Anno, P. (2006), *Rifiuti*, in Dizionario di diritto pubblico, a cura di S. Cassese, Milano, Giuffrè ed.

[8] Dell'Ann,o P. (2003), *Manuale di diritto ambientale*, Padova, Cedam ed.

[9] Farì, A. (2012), Rifiuti: la movimentazione tra fondi dell'azienda non è trasporto, in Diritto e Pratica Amministrativa.

[10] Farì, A. (2016), *Dentro al Collegato ambientale*, focus sui rifiuti –www.quotidianoenergia.it.

[11] Farì, A., Nozione di rifiuto e di sottoprodotto, in (a cura di) Giampietro F. (2011), Commento al D.Lgs 205/2010 sulla gestione dei rifiuti. Profili giuridici e tecnici.

[12] Farì, A. (2011), *Rifiuti: l'Italia si allinea alle direttive comunitarie*, in Diritto e Pratica Amministrativa.

[13] Federici, R. (2006), La nozione di rifiuti: una teoria, in Riv. it. dir. pubbl. comunit..

[14] Feliziani, C. (2011), *Che fine ha fatto il Bel Paese?* Recensione a L. Pinna, *Autoritratto dell'immondizia. Come la civiltà è stata condizionata dai rifiuti*, Bollati Boringhieri, in rivista telematica LABSUS – Laboratorio per la sussidiarietà, *www.labsus.org.*

[15] Feliziani, C. (2012), *Come dare un taglio ai rifiuti?* Recensione a R. Cavallo*, Meno cento chili – Ricette per la dieta della nostra pattumiera,* ed. Ambiente*,* in Rivista telematica LABSUS - Laboratorio per la sussidiarietà, www.labsus.org.

[16] Feliziani, C. (2011), *Emergenza rifiuti: prospettive di amministrazione condivisa,* in Rivista telematica LABSUS – Laboratorio per la sussidiarietà www.labsus.org.

[17] Feliziani, C. (2011), *Prevenire è meglio che smaltire*. Recensione a M. Correggia, Zero Rifiuti, Altraeconomia, 2011, in rivista telematica LABSUS – Laboratorio per la sussidiarietà, www.labsus.org.

[18] Fonderico, F. (2003), *La tutela dell'ambiente*, in S.Cassese (a cura di), Trattato di diritto amministrativo, Parte speciale, vol. II, Milano, Giuffrè ed.

[19] Lee, M. (2011), *EU Environmental Law, Governance and Decision-Making*, Hart Publishing, London, Kramer L., *EU Environmental Law*, Sweet&Maxwell, London,

[20] Lippi, A. (2014), I conflitti territoriali nelle politiche dei rifiuti, Torino, Giappichelli ed.

[21] Liberti, R., *Il distretto industriale sostenibile*, ed. Giannini, Napoli, 2000.

[22] Liberti, R. (2003), Design per la moda, tecnologie e scenari innovative, Firenze, Alinea ed.

[23] Liberti R. (a cura di) (2010), *HIGHWARE L'industria del lusso in Campania*, Camera Nazionale della Moda Italiana, Napoli, Graus ed.

[24] Lucarelli, A., Pierobon A. (2009), *Governo e gestione dei rifiuti. Idee, percorsi, proposte*, Napoli, Edizioni scientifiche italiane.

[25] Massera, A. (2012), *Diritto amministrativo e ambiente*, Ed. Scientifica, Napoli.

[26] Nash, H. A. (2009), The Revised Directive on Waste: Resolving Legislative Tensions in Waste Management?, in *Journal of Environmental Law*, 21(1), pp. 139-149.

[27] RenoSam & Rambøll (2006), The most efficient waste management system in Europe: Waste-to-energy in Denmark.

[28] Rossi, G. (2015), *Diritto dell'Ambiente*, Torino, Giappichelli,

[29] Scotford, E. (2009), *The New Waste Directive – Trying to Do It All ... an Early Assessment*, in Journal of Environmental Law, 11 (2), pp. 75-96.

[30] FA.RE. Fashion Research Lab of the University of Study of Campania Luigi Vanbitelli is a Fashion Lab that work with fashion companies and associationts (Camera Nazionale della Moda Italiana) www.far-lab.com

[31] CIEMME is a fashion company connected to the Fashion Design Master of first level, made in San Marco dei cavoti with che University of Study of Campania, Fashion Design Degree.

Closing the Loop Project

A Research Project by the Designer Francesca Pievani about the Upgrade of Waste Material for Sustainable Innovation in the Fashion Sector

ROSSANA GADDI

Design Department, Politecnico di Milano, Milano, Italy

E-mail: rossana.gaddi@polimi.it

ABSTRACT

Closing the Loop is a research project created by the Italian designer Francesca Pievani, former student of the School of Design of Politecnico di Milano [1] and founder of the brand Fili Pari.[3]

The project arose from the desire to enhance and optimize the resources of the territory of Bergamo through the implementation of a cross-border synergy between different industrial districts (mechanical and textile) of the city of Bergamo area.

The purpose of the project is to incorporate waste materials from the mechanical district into the textile industry by regenerating them, stretching the life cycle of the product waste.

The methodology that led Francesca Pievani into the development of Closing the Loop has been articulated into 3 steps: analysis, research and project.

The analysis, both structured from the statistical-quantitative and the sensitive-qualitative point of view, is based entirely on the Bergamo territory and first examines objective and measurable data, and then sensitive and subjective data relating to habits, customs, culture and the lifestyle of the general population. Thanks to this analysis, it was possible to identify very specific features of the territory of Bergamo, the work culture and Rubber Valley, an industrial district located in the area of Basso Sebino, the world leader in the production of rubber and PTFE (the commonly called Teflon).

The next step was to research and deepen the PTFE and its life cycle, assuming a new employment. Here, the textile industry and the mechanical sector join together in the third step thanks to Closing the Loop: a project to regenerate PTFE waste and to thrive in the textile sector.

In this case it is the process to be the protagonist, rather than the product. The project consists of five different actors: Rubber Valley district, a supposed consortium that manages all the process, a waste regeneration company, a company producing PTFE yarns and finally the textile district of the Seriana Valley. At an experimental stage developed in 2014, the consortium collected and dispatched the scraps to a company that regenerated them, obtaining material from identical properties to the original material. Subsequently, the new material was then organized by the consortium and shipped to another company able to extrude a continuous yarn that through the consortium will be distributed to Seriana Valley District. It was therefore possible to create a 100% PTFE fabric, with which a rhinestone cardigan was created. The yarn used has the same performance as a PTFE block such as heat resistance, solvent resistance, chemical inertia, excellent dielectric characteristics and excellent aging resistance. It was then blended with other yarns such as cashmere, silver wire, lurex, linen and wool to test the potency of PTFE yarn mixed with other yarns and implement the material's performance.

The territory therefore becomes not only a theater but also an actor of a cross-process that calls into question different protagonists (each with a precise and structured role) and contributes to redefining the role of PTFE, which is usually used as a material for the mechanical sector with a new aesthetic and functional purpose.

Keywords: *Waste materials, Fashion design, Design processes, Product lifecycle, Territory enhancement.*

A CLOSE AND NECESSARY CONNECTION WITH THE TERRITORY: WHERE CLOSING THE LOOP STARTS

Closing the Loop was born in Bergamo, speaks about Bergamo, lives in Bergamo: a project created by Francesca Pievani, a young Italian designer born and raised in Bergamo, with a strong passion for her native territory.

The focus of the project is the enhancement of the territory of Bergamo through a cross synergy between different industrial districts strongly connected with the city itself. Starting from the analysis of the territory it has been created a collection of innovative textiles with flavors from Bergamo that would enhance the territory, which stimulate continuous innovation, that represented its essence.

The methodology that led to development of this project has been divided into 3 steps: analysis, research and project. The analysis, structured both from statistical (quantity) and sensitive (quality) points of view, is based entirely on the territory, on its objective and subjective data, on values measurable and sensitive characteristics that led to the identification of the key elements of the territory of Bergamo: the Rubber Valley, the industrial district of rubber and plastic, that is one of the major point of the economic system of the city, but even represents the deep work attitude of its inhabitants.

The second step is represented by the research and analysis of this style: the Rubber

Valley represents a fundamental element of the territory both from the economic and social point of view: it is a global economic power, leader in the world, made up of more than 190 specialized companies that produce mainly rubber seals and in Polytetrafluorethylene, even called PTFE.

The research is focused on PTFE, on its properties and its life cycle, up to hypothesize a new use. Closing the Loop is a project that deals with regenerating the PTFE waste and graft it into the sector fashion knitwear proposing a capsule collection that represents its essence.

The territory becomes not only the mere 'scene' but the 'actor' in a process which joins connects several protagonists (each one with a precise and structured role) and helps redefine the role of PTFE, that from a simple material used in mechanical sector is now interpreted in a new aesthetic and functional key.

The Sebino District of Rubber and Plastic extends over about 80 km^2 and includes 11 municipalities: 10 of the Province of Bergamo and 1 of the Province of Brescia. The sector of specialization of the District it is that of rubber products and gaskets and, for this reason, it is also said Rubber Valley. The origin of the District dates back to the early Fifties with the activity of a local entrepreneur who founded the first seals factory: the Manifattura Italiana Guarnizioni Macchine Colombo in Sarnico (Bergamo), which was followed in the 1954 by Lanza Spa. In those years related to the boom in the automotive industry, they produced seals in asbestos and in iron and copper, taps and fittings of home appliances, but the contemporary evolution in processing of the rubber brought the two leading companies to also produce gaskets in rubber. Large companies have specialized in the production of seals to particular design, going to occupy specs market niches, while maintaining a share of production on the classic seals with standardized O-Ring production, typical of small products companies. In the years immediately following, there will be several employees that set up on their own; already in 1954 the Lanza Spa was founded and for the resourcefulness and foresight of Rag. Antonio Lanza that a path of technological growth started, favored at that time by the development of exceptional polymeric materials (e.g. PTFE) and elastomers (e.g. FKM) which guaranteed high chemical performance. The Italian economic boom of the 60's significantly increased the demand; the need to always produce larger quantities of parts in a short time, forced companies to look for new processes of transformation that would increase the production as well as the quality of the gaskets that were in the meantime become increasingly important components in the various industrial sectors.

It is however in the 70's that begins the true "budding" of new companies, those that today are world leaders; in the Eighties the birth of new businesses, mostly of a family nature initially for then become well-organized companies thanks to the capital of new members investors who begin to glimpse the business in the gaskets sector. Is always in the 80's that the growth of the 'seals chain' begins which is still very active today and decisive in reducing production costs.

The various companies that operate there are specialized exclusively in machining and services complementary to molding. It is possible to summarize them in the following main actors:

- Manufacturers of compounds (raw rubber)
- Printers (molds and equipment)
- Preformers (preparation of raw)
- Deburrers (grating)
- Grinders (finishing/sanding of pieces)
- Sorting machine (visual selection of pieces),

plus various consultants, maintenance and editors hauliers engaged exclusively in this sector. In the 90's and 2000's instead, there is settlement and a consolidation of the existing companies, but also born of artisan printers, often helped from large companies; practically becoming their almost exclusive contractors, helping them stay competitive with emerging Asian countries. Today, the sector undergoes a settlement period but still represents the major National and European manufacturer of seals in rubber and plastic, intended for multiple applications and uses: construction, cars, agriculture, taps, appliances, aerodynamics, food industry.

The framework of the district is mainly composed of numerous companies of small and medium size next to the presence of large industries, presence historically significant with widespread production facilities belonging to major industry-leading multinational groups. In the face of an always constant search for improvement, the district has expanded in the last decade, its production in the plastics sector, and more specifically in PTFE. PTFE, also used in seals, it is progressively replacing the rubber production and redefines the new district structure. The district of the Plastic and Rubber of Sebino in October 2013, according to sources of the Chamber of Commerce of Bergamo and Brescia, counts c.a. 190 companies, as well 4000 employees, with just over a billion euros in annual turnover and 25 millions of euros on average for each company.

WHAT IS PTFE

Polytetrafluoroethylene, commercially known under the names TEFLON®, ALGOFLON®, HOSTAFLON®, FLUON®, is a polymer of tetrafluoroethylene smooth to the touch and resistant to high temperatures. The history of PTFE began in April 1938 in fortuitous circumstances in the Jackson laboratories of the Dupont company.

Around 1930 Ruff and Bretschneider, in Germany, began to study the chemistry of fluorine and obtained the synthesis of gaseous tetrafluoroethylene, for high temperature reaction of HF and chloroform; whose production initially it was only a mere academic interest. In the second in the mid-thirties, Dupont aimed to produce new refrigerants and the chemist Roy J. Plunkett thought of reacting the tetrafluorethylene with acid hydrochloric. Pluckett filled the gaseous TFE metal containers and stored them in dry ice so that the gas could liquefy. On 6 April 1938 the chemist e his assistant noticed that in one of the containers the TFE was cured in the form of a solid white wax; and after some analysis this new material showed particular characteristics. The discovery does not it was immediately exploited by Dupont who understood its real value only thanks to Robert M. Joyce, a young doctorate from the University of Illinois who began experiments that led to effective control of the rapid and explosive polymerization of polymer TFE. Imperial Chemical Industries (ICI) interested in this new material in the early Forties and acquired it soon the rights to produce it. However, in the same period the urgent requests for Teflon of the military sector and the projects of the atomic bomb dismissed the material from the civil market. In 1949 Dupont authorized a new plant for the production of Teflon, but the decisive increase in production occurred in the 1961 with the spread of PTFE-coated cooking utensils. Currently the PTFE polymer is available from several suppliers under a range of names commercial: Teflon for Dupont, Fluon for ICI, Hostaflon for Hoechst, Polyflon for DaikinKogyo, Algoflon and Halon for Ausimont. The Teflon brand was registered in 1945 by Dupont and sold commercially with this name since 1947. The invention of PTFE revolutionized the plastics industry and started applications without limits. In 1990 the president U.S.A. George Bush gave the Dupont National Medal of Technology for the role pioneering of the company in the development and marketing of polymers synthetic.

PTFE is produced by addition polymerization initiated by free PTFE radicals in an aqueous medium under pressure. The polymer obtained, depending on the actual process conditions used, appears in the form of granular resin or aqueous dispersion with a content solid equal to 60-65% by weight. A powdered resin can also be produced through the use of an initiator and an emulsifying agent, when the aqueous medium is stirred moderately. Usually the granules and the powder are used in molding and extrusion processes, while the dispersion is used predominantly for coatings, impregnation and production of compositions loaded with fillers. In general, we get a non-crosslinked polymer with a linear structure, with a high degree of crystallinity and immediately after polymerization and an ability to orientate. The extraordinary characteristics of PTFE® such as chemical inertia, excellent resistance to heat, excellent dielectric characteristics, no hygroscopicity, resistance to solvents and an excellent resistance to aging, are direct consequence of the fluorocarbon structure (consisting only of fluorine and of chlorine), characterized by a high resistance of the main carbononiofluoro bonds and carbon-carbon. Furthermore, the size of fluorine atoms is such that allow the formation of a protective sheath on the carbon atoms that they form the skeleton of polymers, preserving them from chemical attacks. The melting point of freshly polarized virgin PTFE is at 342°C: at this temperature the polymer passes from white solid to transparent gel; such process is irreversible, with an irreversible reduction of crystallinity.

Further analyzes confirm the melting point at 327°C. PTFE also has a dielectric constant (ability to store energy electrostatic versus vacuum) and a dissipation factor (index of how electrical energy is absorbed when the dielectric material is exposed to an alternating electric field) with values among the lowest compared to all solid materials known. This is due to the symmetry of the PTFE structure with respect to fluorine atoms, uniformly distributed along the main chain.

The properties of Polytetrafluorethylene are different than other polymers thermoplastics and deserve a particular deepening: from the point of view chemical, the PTFE is inert towards all known chemical reagents. It comes attacked only by alkaline metals in the elemental state, by chlorotrifluoride and from elemental fluorine to high temperature and pressure.

The PTFE is insoluble in any solvent at temperatures up to 300°C. From a thermal point of view the PTFE has a low coefficient of thermal transmission and is therefore to be considered a thermal insulator; it is not flammable and is stable for indefinitely long times up to 260°C. The PTFE is a material that possesses excellent dielectric qualities in a wide range of temperatures and frequencies. Being the water absorption practically null and void, the characteristics remain unchanged even after prolonged exposure to atmospheric agents. Dielectric strength is not practically influenced by the operating temperature. The resistance to the bow is considerable and the action of the arc does not cause carbon deposits but only vapors do not conductors.

PTFE is used both for products made entirely from this material, both for products composed of compounding of different materials, such as steel, graphite, carbon, molybdenum bisulphide, bronze, glass, and other specials formulations.

CLOSIGN THE LOOP PROJECT: THE USE OF PTFE FOR SUSTAINABLE FASHION

The main applications of Teflon embrace the electrical, mechanical, chemical, medical and homemade. PTFE is used for flexible cables of electronic equipment in the military and aerospace sectors, for sealants, molds, bearings, mechanical tapes and coatings for glass fiber fabrics.

In the chemical industry it is found in gaskets, tanks, pipes, membranes and fiberglass fabric coatings, while in the medical sector the PTFE is used for the production of prosthetics of all kinds, for the replacement of fabrics soft and like suture thread. In the household sector it is used as non-stick in cooking pots. The sector is interesting and not too detailed of clothing, which uses PTFE for laminating or fabric coating high performance technicians. A few years ago, it was launched on the market Teflon® Fabric Protector, a treatment that implements high fabric performance: rejects dirt, stains and splashes from garments without losing weight, appearance, softness, color or breathability [2]. If used for the indoor, it helps to keep upholstery, curtains, linen sheets fresh and clean. Outdoor, Teflon® supplies continuous protection for the upholstery of verandas and terraces, or on the furniture clothes. Fabrics treated with repellents repel resistant dirt, splashes and spray, turning liquids into droplets that slip away. The spots liquids dry easily with a cloth, and just a brushed one remove the dry dirt. PTFE has been used in the field of clothing to implement fabrics and performance, but never it was used as a 100% PTFE fabric because of its difficult nature and composition.

Indeed, PTFE, as a very interesting and high-performance material, and is already under investigation and experimentation in the fashion field.

However, is difficult to deal with it since his behavior differs from other thermoplastic polymers, and so its applications in the field of fashion for a long time have been virtually non-existent. Thanks to continuous experimentation (and the development of new machinery), currently the fashion market is becoming interesting in-depth knowledge of this material, and its hypothetical applications. The Polytetrafluoroethylene is currently used in the field of clothing under three different forms: it is used as a treatment, like expanded membrane, or as a wire.

As a treatment, it represents one protection with "Repel and release" technology called Teflon® Fabric Protector (described before), and that implements and improves fabric performance on to which it applies. In its expanded form instead the PTFE takes the Gore-Tex® name, synthetic fabric with high thermal and waterproof capacity, precisely formed by expanded PTFE. More precisely, it consists of ten Gore-Tex membranes each of which has about 9 billion microscopic holes per square inch. Each hole is about 20,000 times more small of a drop of water, but allows the passage of water vapor produced by human sweating, making the fabric breathable. As a thread on the other hand, PTFE is mainly used as an anti-blister and reinforcing for socks.

The Rubber Valley is a district reality that produces and manages sustained quantities of PTFE, which are mainly used in the sector mechanic. The high production of the material involves a high production of waste that can be recycled in two different ways: mechanical recycling, or chemical conversion of waste materials.

With methods of mechanical recycling of thermoplastic material, they get flakes or granules that will be used to produce new objects. The performance of the recycled material differs from the material of departure because they lose almost half the performance.

Instead, with the Upcycling process, it is possible to maintain the performance of the material because the split and the cleaned molecules will then be combined into a new material.

The Closing the Loop project arose from the need to hypothesize new scenarios life of recycled PTFE, by implementing a process of cross synergy that allows collaboration between different productive districts.

The challenge of this project is represented by the possibility of extending life of the material to give it a new productive life in the textile field.

But how is this system possible?

How the regenerated PTFE can it enter the textile industry?

The heart of the project is in the creation of a system that, thanks to the intervention of several actors, has made possible the processing and the use of PTFE waste of the Rubber Valley in the textile district of the Valle Seriana.

Five actors are involved in the project:

1. Rubber Valley;
2. A Consortium created specifically for the project, which deals with managing and convey the waste of the material;
3. Company that deals with regenerating PTFE waste;
4. Company producing a PTFE yarn;
5. Val Seriana textile district.

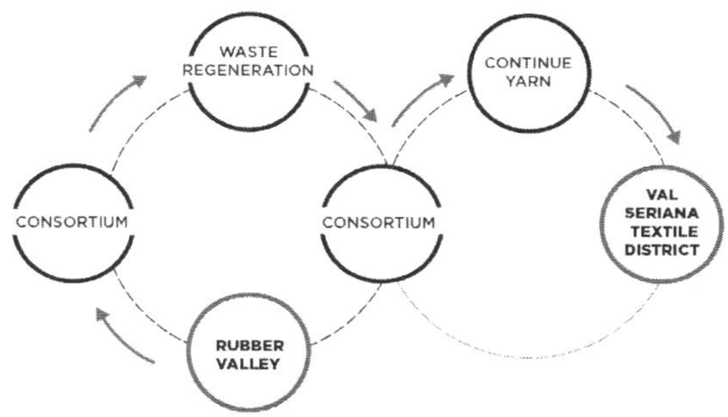

Figure 1: Closing the Loop Project Scheme (Francesca Pievani, 2013)

Initially the Consortium organizes all the PTFE waste from the Rubber Valley and sends them to a center for their regeneration. Here it comes prepared the regenerated material that will be sent to the spinning company. The product obtained is a 100% PTFE yarn, with high technical performances they make an excellent fiber for the fabrics. Then the PTFE thread comes introduced in the Textile District of Val Seriana that can then work it and implement its current market.

The birth of this system could represent an interesting one solution to current pollution issues, including industries of the Rubber Valley are directly responsible. Giving new life to the waste, it will be possible to limit the subsequent production of the material. Moreover, the connection of two different districts of the Bergamo area could be an interesting value generation system: innovation, combined with the experience and know-how of the districts, would make the more competitive and current territory.

The regenerated PTFE yarn represents an innovation both in terms of production and use: it could limit the production of PTFE from the beginning, because the demand on the market would be satisfied by the new material.

This represents an interesting milestone for the Rubber Valley, which will optimize the management of waste (now present in large quantities). Furthermore, the use of the new yarn could also represent an innovation in the fashion system because it is also an interesting solution to the new contemporary textile needs.

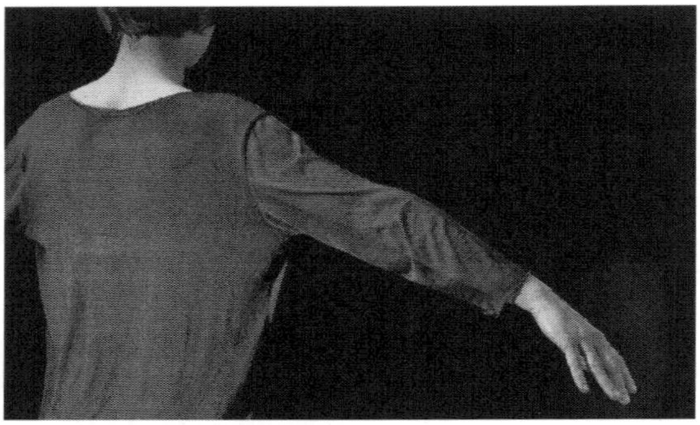

Figure 2: Prototype of 100% PTFE plain knitted cardigan
(Francesca Pievani, 2013)

Its high technical performance makes the yarn ideal for different branch: from sportswear to fashion, from workwear to healthcare, it is possible to use the regenerated material in different combinations, depending on requirements.

First experiments were made on the material, first creating a 100% PTFE knit fabric, as shown in Fig. 2, and then a fabric formed from PTFE yarn mixed with other yarns.

In the Fig. 3 is possible to distinguish the different combinations of untwisted yarns.

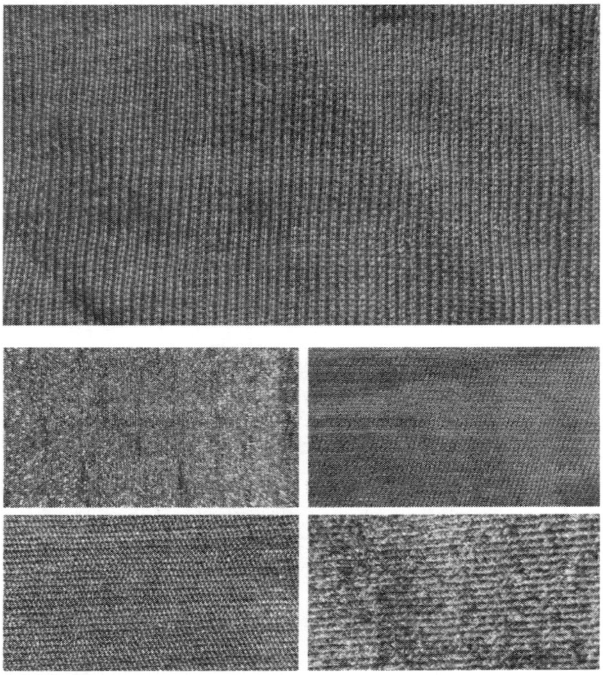

Figure 3: Different Combinations of Untwisted Yarns
(Francesca Pievani with Fili Pari, 2017).

On the left, 100% PTFE fabric, right clockwise: PTFE + Lurex, PTFE + Cotton, PTFE + Gold Yarn, PTFE + Ceramic yarn.

Currently Closing the loop is joined by Fili Pari [3], an Italian fashion design brand created by Francesca and her business partner, Alice Zantedeschi.

Fili Pari promotes and develops a continuous research on materials and fibers, through reinterpretation of the traditional concept of fashion. The aim of the brand is to design garments with highly innovative value, combining research and technology with fresh and everyday style.

REFERENCES

[1] Pievani, F. (2013), 'Closing the Loop. Introduction of PTFE fibers in the fashion knitwear industry like result of a cross synergy between different industrial districts (mechanical and textile) of the territory of Bergamo'. Master Degree Thesis, Politecnico di Milano, Scuola del Design, Design per il Sistema Moda, A.A. Mentor: Prof. Giovanni Maria Conti, Vice Mentor: Proff. Ugo Tinti and Rossana Gaddi.

[2] How Teflon® Fabric Protector works, https://www.chemours.com/Teflon_Fabric_Protector/en_US/benefits/ho w-teflon-textiles-work.htm

[3] © 2017 – Filipari.com. All right reserved.

Waste in Construction Sites, its Transformation and Management in India

TULIKA ROHATGI AND ANJALI AGRAWAL

School of Fashion and Design, G D Goenka University, Sohna Gurgaon Road, Sohna, India

E-mail: tulika.rohtagi@gdgoenka.ac.in; anjali.agrawal@gdgoenka.ac.in

ABSTRACT

Waste is defined as unwanted and unused material, which has been discarded after primary use and can no longer be used. These are generally substances or objects, which are disposed of or are intended to be disposed of by the provision of national law. It is seen that excess generation of waste affects the general health as well as deteriorates the environment. The waste generated in National Capital Region (NCR) has been growing at an alarming rate. It has placed immense pressure on the existing infrastructure that has become a challenge for the municipal bodies responsible for waste management. It is also noted that the construction industries globally account for 40% of greenhouse gases emission with a threat to reverse the current growth trend in developed and developing nations, if measures are not initiated towards curbing them. India is producing nearly 14.5 million tones of construction waste per year, out of which only a fraction is recycled. The objective of study is to understand the key factors in waste management at construction sites, with an idea to reduce, reuse and recycle construction and demolition (C&D) waste. This paper also deals with the innovative methods towards sustainable solution to construction sites on C&D waste management and seeing waste as a resource.

Keywords: *Reduce, Reuse, Recycle, Construction and demolition, Green house gases.*

INTRODUCTION

Construction waste, which is aftermath of construction activity is responsible for more than half of the material used during construction phase of any building. The built environment has been polluted with waste such as earth, pavements and organic material. This waste is known to degrade the land as well as the environment. It is reported that by 2030 about 70% of the buildings will be there in India and rest will still be required to built. There will be a great cost that will grow directly proportional to the construction boom. Thus to reduce this, immediate action is to be taken to reuse and recycle construction waste and make it into a resource.[1]

The Environment Pollution (Prevention and Control) Authority (EPCA) and Centre for Science and Environment (CSE) organized a conference on 'Construction waste to resource' at New Delhi. It became a joint portal which brought together Ministry of Urban Development (MoUD), Bureau of Indian Standards (BIS), Central Building Research Institute (CBRI), National Council for Cement and Building Materials (NCCBM), Building Materials and Technology Promotion Council (BMTPC) with different experts and members of public bodies from different cities. The conference focused on challenges governing construction and demolition of buildings and the solutions to resolve these issues were also discussed.

Waste characterization studies have been conducted by Industrial hygienists, which helped to identify various materials and products posing risk to human health and environment [2]. These materials have been listed as:

- Hazardous wastes
- Asbestos-containing materials
- Lead-containing materials
- Products containing polychlorinated biphenyls (PCBs)
- Solvents, chemicals, petroleum-derived products
- Dust
- Fluorescent and compact fluorescent lamps
- Electronics
- Medical waste
- Materials contaminated with waste

The following materials and products are typically benign:

- Woody and plant materials
- Concrete
- Gravel, aggregate, stone and rock
- Masonry and rubble
- Metals (ferrous and non-ferrous)
- Wood
- Plastic
- Glass
- Doors and windows
- Asphaltic roofing
- Gypsum board

- Carpet and pad
- Cardboard and paper
- Plumbing fixtures
- Lighting fixtures

Figure 1 shows the composition of these materials and products in construction and demolition waste in India.

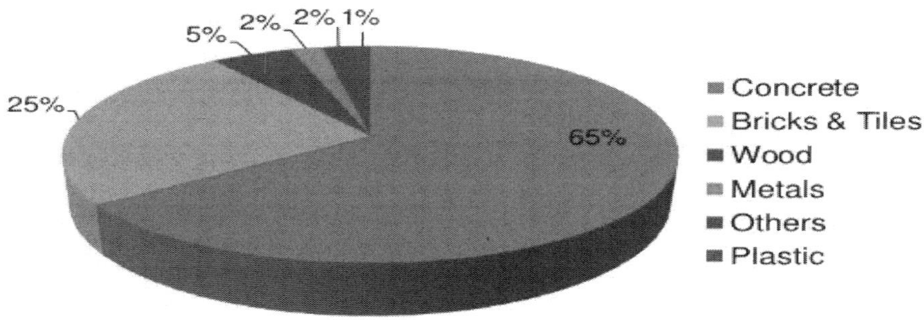

Figure 1: Construction and Demolition Waste in India
(*Source:* Bhattacharya et al., 2013)

Asian Institute of Technology in May 2008 carried out a study to assess the construction and demolition waste in various Asian countries such as Bhutan, Japan, Hong Kong SAR, China, Thialand , India and others [3]. As shown in Figure 2, it was observed that China contributed the maximum waste followed by Japan.

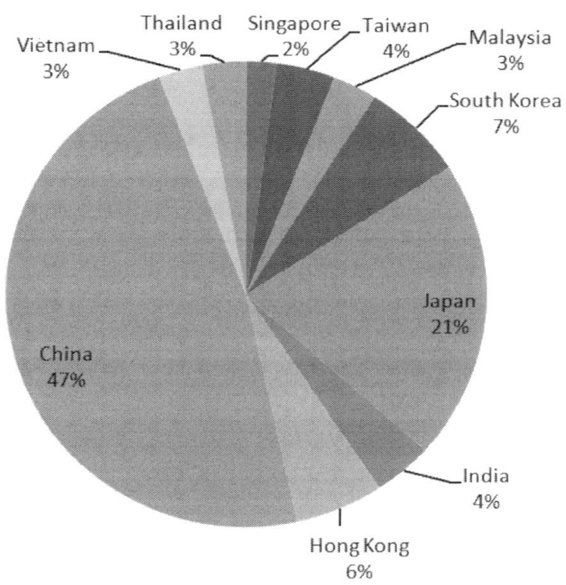

Figure 2: Construction and Demolition Waste in Asian Countries

RELATIONSHIP WITH SUSTAINABILITY

Reduce Reuse and Recycle

The relationship of sustainability with construction and demolition is very dynamic in nature. The concept of sustainability of 3 R which is defined as reduce, reuse and recycle is applied in construction and demolition stage. It means to reduce the use of resources, reusing of raw materials and then utilization of recyclable material more than the usual practice. All the above are applied to entire construction project life cycle starting from design and production of raw material to use, manufacture, transport, dismantle and disposal. This is further defined in hierarchy model as indicated below.

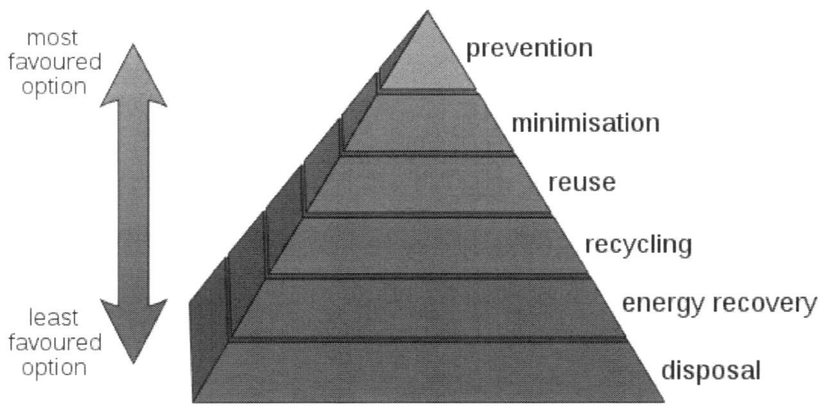

Figure 3: Waste Mangement Hierarchy Model

The waste management hierarchy indicates an order of preference for action to reduce and manage waste, and is usually presented diagrammatically in the form of a pyramid. The hierarchy captures the progression of a material or product through successive stages of waste management and represents the latter part of the life-cycle for each product [4].

Green House Effect

Massive amount of energy is consumed by construction equipment. The process of manufacturing and transporting the equipment as well as the material to the required building site and finally constructing it into the required structure gives out an enormous amount of green house gases and also absorbs a lot of energy. Figure 4 shows the green house emission life cycle.

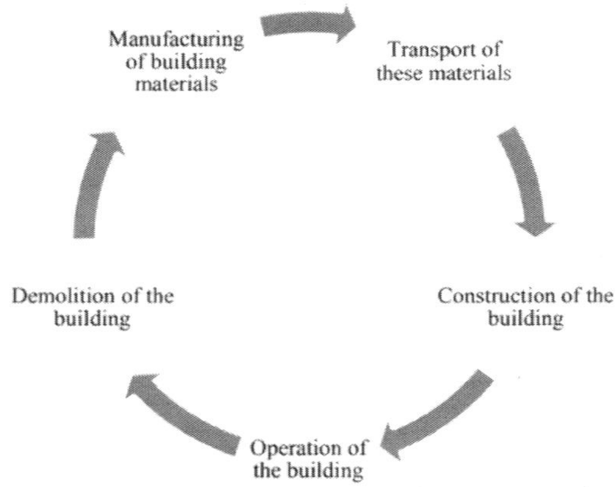

Figure 4: Green House Emission Life Cycle

A case study on Hong Kong was carried out to demonstrate the building construction costs in terms of green house gas emissions. Manufacture of the building material was identified as one of the six greenhouse gas contributor in this study. The others were found to be transportation of building materials and equipment to the site, energy use of the construction equipment, transportation of workers and final disposal of the construction waste.[5] More than half of world energy goes into buildings throughout their lifetime, from construction, through use and finally demolition. They also contribute almost half of the world's carbon dioxide emissions. Total greenhouse gas emissions for a project amount to 6-8%.

Almost 30% to 80% energy is conserved with the adoption of energy reducing methods in both new and existing buildings with commercially available technologies [6]. A study has revealed that during the construction of a building over 80% of the green house gas (GHG) emissions releases. Various energy needs are heating, ventilation, air-conditioning, lighting, telecommunication and entertainment however, the figures in each category may vary from building to building. Material manufacturing and transport sector generally contribute a very small percentage of 10 to 20% of energy consumed in addition to construction, maintenance and demolition.[7] Therefore, the objective should be to target the operational phase of building in order to achieve the greatest reduction in emission.

BUILDING FROM WASTE MATERIALS

Construction and demolition waste accounts for about 30% of all waste generated in India. It consists of numerous materials such as concrete, asphalt, bricks, gypsum,